oPtion$

oPtion$

the secret life of steve jobs
a parody by fake steve jobs

DA CAPO PRESS
A Member of the Perseus Books Group

To L. S., P. B. and M. B.
Much love. Namaste. Peace out.

Copyright © 2007 by FSJ Media LLC

Designed by Jill Shaffer
Set in 11 point Sabon by Eclipse Publishing Services

Cataloging-in-Publication data for this book is available from the Library of Congress.

First Da Capo Press edition 2007
ISBN-10 0-306-81584-2
ISBN-13 978-0-306-81584-3

Published by Da Capo Press
A Member of the Perseus Books Group
www.dacapopress.com

Da Capo Press books are available at special discounts for bulk purchases in the United States by corporations, institutions, and other organizations. For more information, please contact the Special Markets Department at the Perseus Books Group, 2300 Chestnut Street, Suite 200, Philadelphia, PA 19103, or call (800) 255-1514, or e-mail special.markets@perseusbooks.com.

1 2 3 4 5 6 7 8 9—10 09 08 07

While some of this book is based on real events and people, much of the book, including the dialogue, thoughts, and attitudes attributed to characters, is purely fictional and invented by the author to enhance its parody value.

11/07

contents

sometimes I feel like a great chef

sometimes i feel like a great chef
who has devoted his entire life
to monastic study of the art of cooking
& gathered the finest ingredients
& built the most advanced kitchen
& prepared the most exquisite meal
so perfect, so delicious, so extraordinary
more astounding than any meal ever created
yet each day i stand in my window
& watch ninety-seven percent of the world
walk past my restaurant
into the mcdonald's
across the street.

— fsj

prologue

Your average frigtard probably figures I've got it pretty sweet. I'm one of the richest people in the world, and I'm hailed everywhere as the most brilliant businessman of all time. I'm lean and handsome, with close-trimmed hair and a Sean Connery-esque salt and pepper beard. And I'm famous. Like *People* magazine famous. Like everywhere I go people recognize me, and they get all weird around me, and you know what? I love it. I never get tired of it. If there's one thing I can't stand it's retards like Britney Spears who say they wish they weren't famous. Come on. If you really feel that way, then give away all your money, turn your wigger spawn over to Child Protective Services—which, let's face it, is where they ought to be anyway—and move your cottage cheesy ass to a hut in Tibet. What's that? Yeah. That's what I thought. So shut up.

What's even cooler is that I'm not famous for being some steroid-taking action movie star or illiterate dick-grabbing rapper or moronic freak-of-nature basketball player. I'm famous for being a genius, and for running the coolest consumer electronics company in the world, which I totally started in my garage, by myself, or actually with this other guy but he's out of the picture now, so who cares. I'm famous because the devices I create are works of art, machines so elegantly crafted and industrially designed that they belong in a museum. My iMac computers and iLife software restore a sense of childlike wonder to people's lives, and bestow upon their owners a sense that they are more intelligent and even, well, better than other people. I also invented the friggin iPod. Have you heard of it?

People ask me all the time what motivates me. It's not the money. There's already way too much money, so much that I can't even remember how much there is. I never really cared about money anyway. I could wipe my butt with hundred dollar bills, that's how little I care about money. I actually did that once.

To recap: I'm a handsome, famous, spiritually gifted genius; and I wipe my ass with money. No wonder people are jealous of me. I understand. I'd be jealous of me, too. Yet what most people don't realize is that in many ways the life of El Jobso is not always so fantastic. I travel too much. I work too much. I sleep too little. I rarely take a day off. I'll be honest; it's a hard life. It's like Bono always says when we're hanging out, *People think being a rock star is just nothing but sex and drugs and having fun, but it's a grind, man, it really is.*

But the really tough thing about being super brilliant and successful is that people get jealous, and they try to knock you down a peg. In my case the top-seeded jealous frigtard I've ever encountered was a United States Attorney named Francis X. Doyle, a big sweaty blockhead who one day decided that he wanted to run for governor of California and who figured that the best way to launch his career would be to prosecute a high-profile celebrity CEO. Why not, right? Eliot Spitzer worked this same scam, bringing charges against dudes on Wall Street, and now he's governor of New York.

So Doyle and his tiny sidekick, a young lawyer named William Poon (I swear I am not making this up), decided to take down El Jobso. They sat up there in their ugly office in San Francisco, pecking away at their Windows laptops, plotting and scheming, making phone calls to the SEC and leaking information to the press. Fatman and Robin, we used to call them. Or Inspector Clouseau and Kato.

I wasn't their only target. These idiots went after dozens of companies in Silicon Valley. They concocted a fairy tale about greedy executives lining their pockets and cheating investors, and of course the nitwits in the press bought the whole story and ran with it, because let me tell you something, if there's any group of people in the world who are suckers for a story about evil rich people, it's the filthy hacks in the media. These spiteful, hateful, small-dicked losers spend their entire lives in a constant state of jealousy and resentment. Here's their job description: *Interview people who are richer, more successful, and more interesting than you are, then take cheap shots at them in print.* They're parasites. They're leeches. To overcome the shame of what they do, these conniving bastards convince themselves that they're saving the world by exposing all those rich, successful, interesting people as phonies. Which is ridiculous. But whatever.

No doubt you've heard what happened to me. You've read the stories about the big scandal at Apple. The fact is, you've heard only one side. You've heard a distorted tale based on leaks and lies, fabrications and falsehoods created by prosecutors, government flunkies, and media hacks. Now it is my turn. And believe me, my lies and fabrications and falsehoods are way more convincing than theirs.

PART ONE

Trouble in Jobs Land

1

It is Tuesday afternoon. I am barefoot, sitting on a cushion in the lotus position, gazing at a circuit board. This board, no bigger than a playing card, has taken years to create. It is the heart of the iPhone, the most important object my engineers have ever assembled. And it is wrong. I do not know why, exactly. But it is wrong. By this I do not mean that the board does not function correctly. It functions perfectly. But it lacks beauty. My engineers argue that a circuit board need not be beautiful, since no one will ever see it.

"Yes," I say, "but I will know it is there. And I will know that it is not beautiful."

So I have come to the Tassajara meditation room. The room is windowless, white, perfectly silent. I focus on my breathing. I gaze at the circuit board. I allow my mind to empty itself of distraction. Slowly, like a blind man moving along a hallway, I make my way toward the still center, toward nothingness.

I'm almost there when someone knocks at the door. At first I can't believe it. I ignore them. They knock again, and this time they open the door. I turn. It's Paul Doezen and Sonya Bourne, looking grim.

"I'm sorry," Sonya says.

Sonya runs our legal department. She's bony and beak-nosed, high-strung and always freaked out about something.

She's also well aware of our company policy regarding which people can speak to me and under what circumstances. We have ten tiers of access, arranged by rank—the highest people can speak to me by appointment, the mid-tiers can speak to me when I've spoken to them first, and the lowest can never speak to me, and in fact can be fired for trying to speak to me or even for speaking to other people in my presence. Those executives who are allowed to speak to me can do so only during certain time periods, which are arranged into a kind of matrix (certain people have access to more time periods than others) which is available to all of them on iCal under my public folder. It's right there; just sign in, click on my folder, and boom, you can see whether you're allowed to speak to me at the present time, and if not, you can see when your next available window will be. Right now I'm in total black-out mode. No one at Apple is ever allowed to interrupt me when I'm meditating, or doing yoga or tai chi, or getting my weekly high colonic. And when I say never, I mean *never*. Like, if there's an earthquake, or a fire, leave the building and I'll figure it out for myself, once my butt is fully flushed or whatever. But don't even think about taking out that hose before I'm done. Because I'm a total health nut. I'm totally serious about this.

Yet here they are. Breaking the rules.

"It's an emergency," Paul says. He's our chief financial officer, a big fat guy who just joined the company last year. I usually don't hire fat people, just on principle. But he came highly recommended.

"Is the building on fire?"

"No."

"Are we having an earthquake?"

"No." He shakes his head.

"Are there some Goth kids in the lobby with automatic weapons?"

"Huh?"

I hold up my hand. I sigh, dramatically. I close my eyes. It's too late. I've lost my focus. I press my hands together in front of me, and rest my chin on my fingertips—a gesture meant to indicate that I am thinking, even though actually I'm not. At last I get up from the floor and we go down the hall to my office.

"Speak," I say.

Sonya does the talking. I can see her mouth moving, but I'm still so furious about being interrupted that I can't understand a word she says. All I hear is blah, blah, mwah, mwah. But gradually through the din I begin to apprehend that somehow, somewhere, something bad has happened. She's rambling on about stock options and stock prices and government regulators and how all these companies are getting letters raising questions about their accounting. Or something like that.

"That's it?" I say.

"It's important," she says.

"You know," I say, "I'm sure this is all very exciting in your weird little world of numbers and laws and big giant textbooks, but I was *meditating*, do you get it? If you've got some work that needs to be done involving numbers and laws and nasty little people who deal with such things, then go deal with those nasty little people and leave me out of it. That's why I have you here, right? That's *your* job. My job is to make beautiful objects. I cannot do that if I'm disrupted by negative people."

Paul opens his enormous maw and starts to say something and I'm like, "Paul, have you heard of the iPod? You have? Good. Now tell me. Do you want more such beautiful things in your life? Do you want your children to grow up in a world of beautiful objects that do marvelous things? Then leave me alone."

Sonya jumps in and starts explaining how, apparently, sometime way back in the past before iPods were even invented, Apple gave me ten million options, but I never sold them or I never made any money on them or I traded them in for some stock or something. At least I think this is what she tells me. I really don't think about things like options or how much money I have. I'm all about the creativity.

"Sonya," I say, "whatever it is, just do whatever, pay a fine or whatever, but I don't want to spend a minute on this. I didn't want to hear about it."

Yet when I open my eyes she's still there. I'm stunned. She says she doesn't think I understand. People are talking about criminal charges. She says the way we gave out options was we dated them so they were granted on days when the stock price was low, so that whoever got the options made an instant profit. Apparently at one time this was considered okay, or maybe not, but in the old days nobody cared, but then some idiots in Washington changed the laws because of Enron and now they're going around busting people.

"Steve," she says, "this is serious. The SEC is sending lawyers here and they're going to go through our books. The U.S. Attorney has contacted us too. Some of these backdated options went to you. Do you understand?"

"No, I do *not* understand, and look, I'm not stupid. Just because I didn't finish college doesn't mean you have to speak to me like I'm a child. I could understand this if I wanted to. I just don't want to. So just take it out of my bank account or whatever. Jesus. Do I have to do everything for you guys?"

"Well, paying a fine would be one scenario."

She looks at me.

I'm like, "Dude, what? Spit it out."

"Well," she goes, "some people are facing criminal trials. Some people might be going to . . . well, in some cases, certain charge may carry potential penalties that could include fines or even, possibly, in some scenarios, the possibility of incarceration."

That's a strange word, *incarceration,* and after she says it a weird silence comes over the room. Suddenly the air feels really,

really cold, and it's so quiet that I can hear the air conditioning whirring in the walls, and I'm thinking to myself, *Holy friggin mother of Jesus, I am so going to* kill *the a-holes who did the HVAC work in this place.* Because I specifically told them I want this place *silent.* Not *quiet.* Silent. Like a friggin tomb, I told them. Yet there's this whirring in the walls as if we're up in a jet at thirty thousand feet. How am I supposed to concentrate? This is how I'm supposed to work? I can't even hear myself think.

Paul stands there, sweat beading on his monstrous forehead, his chest still heaving from the exertion of walking down the hall ten minutes ago, or maybe from the extremely hard work of having to stand up instead of sitting down. He won't even look at me; instead he's taking a great interest in the carpet, which, to be fair, is an exquisitely soft carpet that was hand-woven, hand-tufted and hand-dyed by master Tibetan craftspeople who are living in exile in Nepal. It's based on one of my designs.

Then it dawns on me, and I'm like, "Wait a minute! You assholes! Oh, God, I friggin *hate* you guys! I'm being punked, right? Where are the cameras? Where's Ashton? Dude, get out here! I friggin hate you, you a-hole! Oh man, you guys are soooo gonna get nailed for this one, I'm not even kidding, I'm gonna call Larry Ellison and we are totally going to cook something up, you better watch your friggin backs!"

But they just stand there giving me this pitiful look. They look the way people do when they're about to have their dog put to sleep, or when they've been to visit someone in this hospital who's terminally ill and they don't really want to be in the hospital looking at all the freaky machines and smelling that skanky stale hospital smell and it takes all their strength just to stand there and smile and make small talk, and then at last they've fulfilled their obligation and it's over and they can rush outside and breathe fresh air again and feel the sunshine on their faces, thinking, *Man oh man, there but for the grace of God go I, right?*

Yeah, it's just like that. Either the dog thing or the terminally ill hospital visit thing. Or maybe a mix of both.

"Steve," Sonya says, "we're not punking you. I promise. Do you know what it means when the SEC says it wants to investigate you?"

"As a matter of fact," I say, "I don't. But let me ask you something. Do you know the rule about interrupting me when I'm meditating?"

"I'm aware of the policy," Sonya says.

"You're aware. Okay. Good. So here's what I'd like you to do. I'd like you both to leave this room and go back to your offices and fire yourselves. Okay? Thank you."

They leave. I go back to the Tassajara room and resume meditating. Within ten minutes I've forgotten that I ever spoke to them.

But that evening, after dinner, as I'm doing my digestion yoga, I get a call from Tom Bowditch, our biggest shareholder. Tom is also a member of our board of directors. He says we're having an emergency meeting of the board on Sunday to discuss this situation with the SEC.

"I'm pretty sure you're supposed to ask my permission if you want to have a board meeting," I say.

He growls. I'm not kidding. Like a dog. He says, "Just be there, you fuckwit," and hangs up.

I'm not sure, but I'm guessing from his tone that maybe there really is something to be concerned about.

2

"**Sure I know** about the SEC inquiry. They're going after every-body," Larry Ellison says. "It's a witch hunt. A hundred compa-nies got letters."

We're at his Japanese Zen palace in Woodside, walking along a carefully raked gravel path beside the man-made pond in the Japanese garden. We both wear formal tea-ceremony kimono, in black, and wooden sandals. Birds are whistling in the trees. These are special teeny-tiny bonsai birds that Larry imports from Japan. They don't fly away because he feeds them special Japan-ese bird food.

"Some U.S. Attorney wants to run for governor, and now the asshats from the SEC are jumping in too. These are pygmies, Steve. These are guys who spent all that money to go to law school and now they're making a hundred and fifty grand and they can't afford to buy a house in the Bay Area. Meanwhile they see all these freako engineers with Asperger's syndrome driving Ferraris. For this they blame guys like you and me, because we've committed the great sin of creating jobs and generating wealth. We've spawned a valley full of obnoxious nerd millionaires, and the lawyers hate us for it. And you know what? I don't blame them. Look at us. Thursday afternoon and we're dressed like Japanese warlords and having a tea ceremony. I'd hate us too."

This is one area where Larry and I disagree. I agree that people hate us, but I don't believe the hatred is justified. Larry, on the other hand, is a very insecure guy. He's way too nice. His company, Oracle, has been in business for thirty years, and during that time its software has done more to improve the world than almost any other product I can think of. Plus Oracle has enriched its business partners and gone out of its way to treat its customers with care and respect.

To be sure, Larry doesn't pull too many eighteen-hour days at Oracle anymore. But that's because he's so busy helping out in soup kitchens and animal shelters and halfway houses for homeless disabled kids born to crack-addicted mothers. Don't look for any stories on that stuff, though.

Nobody knows about Larry taking in stray cats and dogs and giving them a home on his compound in Woodside. Nobody knows about Larry's philanthropic work. He just shows up at the soup kitchen, dishes out the food, and disappears. He doesn't go looking for praise. He doesn't need it. The good karma has come back to him, however. He's the eleventh-richest guy in the world, a mega-billionaire. Naturally the money is the only thing the media ever wants to talk about. They just love to reduce people to caricatures.

In my case it's different. First of all I'm only the one hundred and thirty-second richest person in the world. Moreover, my wealth is deserved. Name one person from the past hundred years who has made a bigger contribution to the world than I have. See what I mean?

We're strolling past a shallow part of the pond, admiring Larry's exotic koi fish, when Larry begins telling me some ancient Japanese fable about some warlord who was this great and gifted leader and yet his kingdom was destroyed because he had this single tiny flaw. He rattles on and on and on and finally I tell him, "Larry, for the love of Buddha, would you please get to the point?"

"The point," he says, "is that maybe there's no truth to any of these charges, but it doesn't matter. It's a shakedown. It's one big ass-fucking gangbang, and you're the pivot man, sitting in the middle, getting three hundred and sixty-degrees of corn-holing."

"You know what I love about you, Larry? You always cheer me up."

"It's the lawyers. They're evil. They're bloodsuckers. They're parasites. We create wealth, they live off our scraps. They see guys like us with money, and they say, 'Okay, let's invent some law that fucks this guy up. Let's create some rules about accounting that are tricky and complex and arcane that nobody can possibly comply with them. Then let's bribe some Congressmen to pass the law, and we'll shake these rich bastards down.' That's what it is. You pay to settle the case, and the lawyers split the money. They're all in on it together—not just the plaintiff lawyers but your own defense lawyers too. At the end of the day it's no different than if they put a gun to your head and robbed you in an alley. It's a mugging. Same damn thing. Like it or not, this will only end one way—you will write a huge check, and these fuckers will fight over it like a pack of hyenas tearing at a deer carcass."

"Dude," I say, "I'm pretty sure hyenas don't eat deer. I don't think they even have deer in Australia or whatever."

"Doesn't matter. The point is, in a perfect world we wouldn't have to deal with this shit. If we were living in feudal Japan, guys like you and me would command our own armies. We'd have these bastards from the SEC strung up by their nuts and we'd shove hot pokers up their poop chutes. And isn't this the way things should be? Shouldn't society recognize that people who are able to amass great fortunes have proven themselves to be superior, and therefore should be allowed to rule?"

"I have to admit, it makes sense when you say it."

"Sure it does. And I've got more bad news for you. You've got a leaker. Everyone in the Valley is talking about this. Everyone knows you got a letter. Just thought you should know. You also should know how much people are loving this. I mean *loving* it. I had no idea how much people out here hated you. Did you? They hate you a lot."

"That's nice to know."

"It *is* nice to know," Larry says. "Means you're doing something with your life. You want to be remembered as a nice guy? A guy everyone liked? No thanks. You're the guy who saved Apple when nobody believed it could be done. That pisses people off. Great. Wonderful."

Larry knows all about being hated. People think he's just some narcissistic super-obnoxious *nouveau riche* asshole. It's easy to see him that way, with his gigantic yachts, the World Cup sailboats, the fighter jets, the Zen palace. And sure, he's had too much plastic surgery. Not as much as that lady who looks like a giant cat. But too much. He's addicted to it. He's had two face lifts and nobody knows how many eye jobs.

But the fact is that beneath all that Larry is a kind and generous soul. He is probably the closest thing I have to an actual friend. For one thing we're both orphans. We've both got that orphan gene that says, "You think you can abandon me? Well, I'll make you pay attention; I'll make you regret giving me up."

"Here's my advice, take it or leave it," Larry says. "Remember your Sun Tzu. Avoid confrontation with a strong opponent. To win without fighting is best. Come on. Let's eat."

Larry's teahouse sits on an island in the center of the pond and is an exact replica of the seventeenth-century Shokintei teahouse in Kyoto, only slightly larger than the original. (Ahem.) There are tatami mats on the floor, paper window screens, a wall that slides open to a view of the pond. Larry's imported tea servants, these very hot Japanese geisha girls, show us in and begin the ceremony.

At Larry's place the tea ceremony takes four hours. It's the full hoo-ha, with crazy food and ten kinds of tea, plus geisha girls doing song-and-dance numbers. After the meal, Larry gets up and shows off his karate moves, which scares the shit out of the geisha girls. They all go running from the room screaming.

By the time we're done it's five in the afternoon. From Larry's driveway we can see out over the entire Valley. Low black clouds are massing overhead, getting ready to pour. Up here in the hills a few fat drops have started splattering down.

"All those poor bastards," Larry says, nodding toward Route 280, where the traffic is jammed up and inching along. "They have no idea what's about to hit them."

"It's just a rain storm."

"I'm talking about the SEC thing. You remember the quake in '89? You remember where you were right before everything started shaking?"

"All they're doing is sending out letters."

"Just wait until people start getting arrested. Wait till stocks start getting slaughtered. You're going to see market caps cut in half. You'll see billions of dollars wiped out overnight. We're not talking about a few rich assholes paying some fines. We're talking about all these poor bastards out there on the highway having their retirement funds wiped out and their savings destroyed. Then come the layoffs. This is bad, Jobso. This is big and bad and scary and endemic. This is going to hurt everyone in the Valley. It's like the war on terror, and we're the terrorists."

"Larry," I say, "I love you, but I think you're being a little melodramatic here."

He takes me by the shoulders. He looks me straight in the eyes, and he's not smiling.

"Listen. Listen to me. Don't mess around with these guys. Don't fight them. Just settle. No matter how much money they want, just pay the bastards and move on. Sign a confession, do whatever you have to do."

3

Tom Bowditch has a seat on our board because ten years ago, when we were almost dead, he bought a huge chunk of our stock and got himself elected to a director's position. He's seventy-three years old and has spent most of his career as a corporate raider. He's obnoxious, abrasive, and almost universally hated, especially by people on the Apple board. He also happens to be about the size of an eighth-grader, which is why behind his back we call him "boy's dick." He has jet-black hair slicked straight back and wears Old Spice aftershave. He went to Yale and never fails to mention this. Many years ago he was deputy something or other at the CIA, and he's wired in with all sorts of shadowy people in Washington. He lives in Las Vegas in a penthouse on top of a casino, and flies a Gulfstream IV, which is not quite as sweet as my Gulfstream V, but still plenty nice.

Having Tom on our board is like owning a Rottweiler. He's great protection, but you never know when he might lose his marbles and turn on you. Basically, Tom scares the crap out of me. Especially when he's yelling at me, as he is right now, in front of the entire management team and board of directors, saying, "Jesus fucking Christ, kid, every time I turn my fucking back you end up sticking your dick in a fucking blender and I gotta fly out here and get you un-fucked. You know who you're like? You're like fucking Rain Man. You ever seen that movie? With the retard who's also a genius? That's you, kid. You're a genius, in your own way, I'll give you that. You've got immense fucking gifts. But godfuckingdammit you are also one hell of a fucking retard sometimes, you know that?"

I'm not even kidding. This is exactly how Tom talks. To make it worse, there's spit spraying out of his mouth, and his breath smells like a tub of something you might find sloshing around on the bottom shelf in a morgue.

It's Sunday morning and Tom is running the board meeting. He's flown in from Vegas wearing a black satin track suit. Supposedly he owns fifty of these, plus fifty navy blue suits. He has them custom-made by some famous tailor in Hong Kong.

"Ladies and gentlemen," Tom says, "let me introduce you to the enemy."

He clicks a button on his Apple remote—small, sleek, perfectly balanced—and boom, like that, without a pause, a photo appears on the wall screen.

It's a big fat-faced Irish-looking guy with thinning hair, no neck and moronic eyes. Staring straight into the camera, not smiling. I hate him already.

"This is Francis X. Doyle. He's the U.S. Attorney for the Northern District of California. He wants to put all of us in jail."

Tom waits a moment to let that sink in. Everyone stares at the screen, at that big fat stupid Irish face.

"And here's his top assistant," Tom says, pulling up a photo of an Asian dude who looks like a fourteen-year-old in a suit and a pair of black nerd glasses. "William Poon. That's right, *Poon*. As in the word that goes before tang. Don't be deceived by his appearance. He's a fucking animal. First in his class at Harvard Law, clerked for a Supreme Court justice, and has a total hard-on for Apple ever since his iPod battery crapped out after ten months and you dickheads refused to replace it under warranty."

"Our iPod batteries last longer on average than batteries in any other music player," I say.

"I'm just saying," Tom says. "The kid is tough. Don't underestimate him. And whatever you do, don't make fun of his name, unless you really want to piss him off. Apparently he goes nuts.

19

Took a lot of shit for it at Harvard. Okay. Here, meanwhile, are the other bad guys."

He clicks through a series of photos of some dweebs in drab gray suits. These are lawyers from the SEC. From what Tom says they're basically mindless, nameless, interchangeable bureaucrats, like the agents in *The Matrix*. They're going to go through our books and look for mistakes, and most likely they'll find something, because they always do, and we'll have to pay a fine, and we'll get hit with shareholder suits. The usual stuff. No big deal. The problem, Tom says, is Doyle. Doyle can do more than charge you a fine. He can put you in jail. And this is something he wants very much to do.

"He wants to run for governor," Tom says. "He figures he can make a name for himself by putting a few big names behind bars."

Tom's idea is that we should conduct our own investigation. This makes us look like we're taking this seriously and doing our best to get to the bottom of it. But it also lets us control the pace.

"We need to get out ahead of this thing," he says.

Tom has retained a team of lawyers to do the job. He brings them in and introduces them. The one in charge is about sixty years old, with gray hair and very scary Paul Newman–style steel blue eyes. His name is Charlie Sampson, and according to Tom he's an expert in securities law and also a former federal prosecutor.

"Best of all, he's a Yalie," Tom says. "After Harvard Law School, he clerked at the Supreme Court, and then spent fifteen years as a prosecutor, during which time he put a Congressman in jail. In other words, Charlie knows how guys like Doyle think. He's a valuable quarterback to have on our team."

Sampson gets up and thanks Tom for the kind words and then makes his presentation, introducing himself and the three guys who work for him and telling us about some past cases where they've helped companies deal with similar situations. His assistants are clean-cut Ivy League types with expensive haircuts and button-down shirts. Sampson tells us their names, but I'm unable to pay attention, because as Sampson is speaking, to my absolute horror, one of the young guys takes out a Windows laptop, which, at Apple, is about on the same level of etiquette as leaping up on a table at lunch and taking a crap in the veggie dip.

I'm staring at him, aghast. The guy stares back at me, as if to say, "So, what are you gonna do about it?" I believe he is doing this intentionally to provoke me. There's a twinkle in his eyes. I want to walk down there and rip his head off. But I don't. I don't even say anything. I look away and take deep breaths through my nose and silently chant my mantra until I can regain my composure.

When I'm finally able to speak I say, "Tom, dude, I appreciate you going to all the trouble to line up these fine lawyers and everything, but it really seems to me that having these guys around could become a significant distraction, and seriously, dude, I don't see that some letter from the SEC actually merits such a big response."

"First of all," Tom says, "this *is* serious. Second, don't call me *dude*. I've told you before. Don't make me tell you again."

"Whatever, dude. But just because you woke up with sand in your crack I don't think you need to fly in here and hassle us. But whatever. You go ahead. I need to get my harmony back."

Then I lean back in my chair and close my eyes and pretend I'm meditating, as if to say, *Hey, asshole, wake me up when you're done having your tantrum.* It's what I always do when people get angry. The crazier they get, the more I go Zen. It drives them nuts. To be honest I'm about *this* close to just getting up and leaving, because the last thing I need on a Sunday morning is to be sitting here getting sprayed with spit and seeing my own boardroom—which I designed myself, as a personal homage to Walter Gropius—being polluted by the stink of Windows laptops. Moreover, everyone here knows that Sunday morning is my Ultimate Frisbee league and nothing, I mean *nothing,* messes with my Ultimate. It's sacred. To show that I am here under protest, I'm wearing the uniform of the Apple Ultimate Frisbee team—black shorts, black socks, black shoes, and a black mock turtleneck T-shirt with a tiny black Apple logo silkscreened on the shirt, a half shade darker than the shirt itself, so that you can barely see it. In other words, *classy.*

Also here under protest is Lars Aki, our head of design, who is wearing a wet suit and little rubber booties to remind everyone that he's supposed to be kite-boarding right now. He's sitting in an Eames chair with his leather-bound sketch pad, looking out the window at the trees bending in the wind and no doubt thinking how awesome the chop is up on the bay today and getting more and more bummed out.

Will MacKenzie, who's on the board because he's my pal, jumps in and says he agrees with me that we shouldn't let this options business become too big a distraction to our product development. Some other guy who's on the board and whose name I can never remember—he's about ninety years old, and runs a clothing company, or a chain of clothing stores, something like that—says he agrees with Will MacKenzie.

Al Gore, who's joining by videoconference using our incredible iChat AV software, pipes up and says in his stupid drawl, "Say, if you folks don't mind, I'd like to talk a little bit about what Apple can do regarding this climate change crisis that we're facing."

"Request denied," Tom says.

"What's that?" Gore says. "I'm sorry, I missed that."

Tom mutes the computer with Gore's face on it and turns his attention to Zack Johnson, the only member of the board who hasn't spoken yet. Zack was our CFO when this accounting stuff took place. He left last year to run a hedge fund, but I kept him on our board because he always does whatever I tell him.

"Zack," Tom says, "I expect you'll get involved here, and work with Paul Doezen and help him find any information that's needed. And Sonya, I'd like you to make sure that Charlie and his team get all the support they need."

That's when Sonya drops the bombshell. "Actually," she says, standing up, "since the company has gone against my recommendation and decided to retain outside counsel, I'm going to resign. Effective immediately."

She slides a letter across the table. Tom looks at the letter.

"You can't quit in the middle of an SEC investigation," he says.

Sonya doesn't bother to respond. She looks at Sampson and says, "If you need anything from me you can call my lawyer."

"You've hired a fucking lawyer?" Tom says. He looks like smoke is going to start pouring out of his ears. "Where do you think you're going? Sit back down, lady. Did you hear me?"

Sonya walks out. After that the meeting breaks up. I'm halfway out the door, hoping to catch the end of the Ultimate game, when Tom grabs my arm, tight enough that it hurts, and says, "Hold on. I need to talk to you."

4

"Kid," he says, in a low voice, "it's just you and me here now, okay? So I need you to tell me the truth. People get greedy. It happens. It's human nature. These guys, Charlie Sampson and his guys, they're good. If there's a problem, they're going to find it. So tell me. Are they going to find something?"

We're in the conference room, alone, with the door shut. He's leaning close to me. I can smell his Old Spice, which makes me queasy.

"This company," I say, "operates under the highest standards of integrity and honesty and transparency. These have been our principles from day one."

"Jesus. It's worse than I thought. Fuck." He slugs down the end of his coffee. "Kid, you do understand what it means when your general counsel quits and hires her own lawyer, right?"

I inform Tom that earlier in the week I instructed Sonya to fire herself, so it could be that she was just following my orders.

He makes this sound that's halfway between a groan and a sigh. He tells me he's done some asking around and discovered that the guys who are really running this investigation are way above Doyle; it's all coming out of Washington. "This goes right to the top," he says. "These people want your head on a platter."

I ask him what people he's talking about. He says he'll answer my question with a couple of questions of his own, which are: (a) which political party do I make a big deal of supporting every four years during the presidential elections? and (b) which political party actually won the last two elections?

Fair enough. The fascists in Washington hate me because I'm a super liberal lefty Democrat. It drives them nuts because, unlike the big oil companies, out here in Silicon Valley guys like me manage to make a lot of money without resorting to being evil and exploiting people.

"The problem," Tom says, "is that you gave them an opening. You see? These guys hate you, and you gave them something to attack you with. It's like when Clinton got the blowjobs."

"I didn't get any friggin blowjobs. Jesus. I wish."

"I'm speaking metaphorically," he says.

Tom says that when you know you're in the public eye you've got to be a total friggin Boy Scout. This applies not only to blowjobs but to compensation and accounting. He says it's one thing to be a really highly paid executive, and another to be the kind of creep who cooks the books in order to get a little bit more than he's supposed to.

"There's an old expression where I grew up," he says. "Pigs get fat, hogs get slaughtered. Ever heard that?"

"Dude, I grew up in California, okay? Not on some friggin pig farm."

He makes that groaning sound again, and heads for the door.

"I'll be in touch," he says.

On the bright side, I arrive in time to catch the end of the Ultimate game, and we totally beat the snot out of some chiptards from AMD.

5

People often ask me how I feel about drugs. My stance on this is a little bit controversial. I like drugs. I think they're good. Fair enough, not heroin. And not cocaine or crack or crystal meth. But soft drugs, like marijuana and hashish, and the psychedelics, like LSD and peyote, I think are really beneficial both on an individual level and a cultural level. Frankly, I think marijuana is what got us out of Vietnam. In my own life, drugs have played a huge role not only in helping me relax and unwind and have a good time, but also in being able to open up my creativity and see things in a new way. Without marijuana, I can almost guarantee you, there would have been no Apple Computer. Certainly there would have been no Macintosh.

As I see it the problem began with Nancy Reagan and her "Just Say No" campaign. Yes, it was stupid. But it worked. They've succeeded in scaring an entire generation away from drugs. You should see the kids who come through Apple for interviews. Ask them if they've ever done acid and they give you this look like you just asked them how many times they've been abducted by aliens. This shunning of drugs has produced a generation of conformists. Look at all these new companies in the Bay Area, all these supposed "tech" companies. God knows what they do, but it's all some variation on the same theme and they all have names like Zizzl and Drizzl and Dazzl, so you can't tell them apart. Can't these kids think of anything original? Apparently not. My theory is it's because they've never used psychedelics.

Thank you, Nancy Reagan. Thank you, Christian Right zealots. You've ruined an entire generation. These kids grew up with parents who were terrified to let them go outside and play without being supervised. Then they got to school and got hit with the AIDS education stuff, and I know it's important to teach kids to fuck safely, but come on. Let's be honest. They're really using this to scare kids about sex itself. And it's worked wonders. It's very effective. These kids are terrified—of drugs, of sex, of each other.

Kids, I'm sorry, but the truth is, a few evenings spent sleeping with strangers and tripping your brains out on peyote or some really clean blotter acid would be the best thing that could ever happen to you. Forget trying to get a job at Google or trying to raise venture funding for some startup. Go down to the Mission and score some weed. Buy yourself a bong, and fire it up. *Then* go think of an idea for a company.

Which is all a long way of saying that the first thing I do when I get home from the Ultimate Frisbee game is go upstairs to my office, put on some Leonard Cohen and fire up a bowl of some fine reddish buds. It's mellow stuff, seventies-style weed, not this whacked out paranoia-inducing hydroponic stuff that they grow today, this stuff that makes you want to crawl under your bed and hide. I have my weed grown specially for me by a guy up in Oregon who knows how to keep the THC content low. Really, really nice stuff.

I'm just feeling a glow when the phone rings and it's Larry Ellison telling me to turn on the TV, which in my case is an incredibly huge super-high-resolution plasma display which won't hit the market for another two years.

There on CNN is Jeff Hernandez, a friend of ours, being perp-walked out of his house in Woodside by federal agents. The whole thing is being filmed from a helicopter. I can't believe it.

Jeff is the CEO of Braid Networks. He has a wife and four kids. He goes to church.

The dick from Fox says Jeff is being charged with twelve counts of fraud.

"They're rounding up some others too," Larry says. "His CFO, his general counsel, couple of board members. All this over some paperwork. Couple of accounting mistakes. Buddy, this is worse than I realized. This is some bad shit, brother."

After we hang up I turn off the TV and go out to the backyard. I try to do some T'ai Chi, but my legs are shaking so badly that I can't hold a position.

Okay, so I'm scared. I know what you're thinking, but no, it's not the butt rape. Not because I'm a huge fan of being butt-raped. But the butt rape, I am pretty sure, takes place mostly in your more hardcore Oz-type penitentiaries where you get the truly criminal gang-type people. Not to be biased against any certain ethnic or socioeconomic groups, because I am a very serious Buddhist and not at all a racist or a bigot of any kind, and as you know if you've seen our ads we are all about using people of color to sell products, so it's not at all that I think white people are better or anything. But let's face it, if you put a bunch of rich white businessmen on some minimum security prison farm, they're not going to butt-rape each other. They'll wait till they get out and do it to each other metaphorically, like they always have.

What really scares me is being tossed out of my company. This happened to me once before, back in the eighties. Apple hit a rough patch, and they blamed all the problems on me. Getting fired nearly killed me. I literally thought I was going to die.

My shrink says it's because I'm an orphan. He says that being rejected by my birth mother inflicted damage on my soul.

"It carved this pit into you," he says, "this giant hole that you can never fill, no matter how much you accomplish. You need to prove to your birth mother that she made a mistake when she gave you away. So you work and you work and you work. You never stop. But no matter what you achieve, it's never enough to fill that hole. And yet you can't stop, either. Because if you do, you die. That's how it feels. You'll cease to exist. You'll be nothing. Nobody. You'll be that little boy, hiding under the bed, the day you learned you were adopted and you wished you could become invisible. If you lose your job, your birth mother wins, and you lose. She was right, and you were wrong. She was right to give you away."

It seems to me that for two hundred and fifty bucks an hour the guy could go a little easier on me. But anyway, he's right. That's how it feels. Like I'll die. It terrifies me.

Yes, I survived the last time Apple threw me out. But this time, I'm not so sure. I'm fifty-one years old. I've had cancer. I'm not as tough as I used to be.

And even the last time nearly killed me. I was thirty years old and living by myself in a mansion in Woodside with no furniture, just a huge stereo system and pillows on the floor. For months I did nothing. I'd take acid for days on end. The record was fourteen days, and believe me, that was a life-changing episode. But mostly it was this Keebler-Kahn type period in my life, with the eight stages of mourning, like anger, denial, anger again, then more anger, then rage, vindictiveness, more anger, and then revenge.

That's when the healing could really begin, once I'd set out to get revenge on these butt-munchers who'd tossed me out. I hired away Apple's best engineers and started a company called NeXT whose goal was to create the most amazing computer in the world. We did it. But there was one problem: The machines cost ten thousand bucks each. Nevertheless, when Apple started tanking without me, and the board of directors came begging for me to return, I brought with me the software from those NeXT machines. That software became the foundation of our new Macintosh computers. It saved Apple.

Since then I've bestowed upon the world other glorious devices and programs that restore a sense of childlike wonder to people's lives. I invented the iPod, in all its incarnations, and the iTunes music store. I've created a hi-fi music system and a device for playing movies on your TV. Soon I will deliver the finest telephone ever created.

What happens to the world if the Jobsmeister is suddenly taken out of the game? Let me give you a hint: Microsoft. Yeah. It's scary.

At midnight the phone rings and it's Larry again and I can tell by his voice that he's even more baked than I am. He says six executives from Braid were picked up, plus two venture-fund guys who sit on the board—Barry Lunger from Greylock and Peter Michelson from Menlo.

"Those two I can see," Larry says. "Pair of first-rate shitbags."

He pauses to do a bong hit. He's got this incredible collection of bongs. He buys them on eBay. One is from the sixties and supposedly was used by Jerry Garcia.

"So I was thinking," Larry says, "of a way to take your mind off things." He starts snickering like an idiot, the way he does when he's stoned. "You ready? Are you? Okay. Two words: *Rat Patrol.*"

I sigh. "Oh, man, come on. I'm working."

Which is a lie. I'm actually reading *Siddhartha* for the thousandth time. But whatever.

"Steve, seriously. It'll be awesome."

Rat Patrol is what Larry calls it when we drive his Hummer up to the city and cruise the Tenderloin in the middle of the night, wearing balaclavas and commando outfits and firing Super Soakers at transvestite hookers. You get points for how many you hit, with bonuses for letting them get as close as possible to the Hummer before you leap through the roof and open fire. We've done it a few times and I'll admit, it's pretty fun, especially when the trannies get all pissed off and start shouting and swearing. Larry aims for the face, and tries to blow their wigs off.

We learned this game from Arnold. He and Charlie Sheen invented it in Los Angeles with a couple of other guys. They call it Commando. But we started calling it Rat Patrol because we were hanging out the back of Larry's Hummer like the machine gunner in the old *Rat Patrol* TV show.

How we heard about it is that one time Arnold was up in the Valley visiting T.J. Rodgers and the two of them took us along. Arnold uses paint guns instead of water cannons, which frankly I think is a little bit cruel, because those paint balls really sting when they hit you. The water cannons seem kinder.

Anyway, Arnold says we've got *carte blanche* on this stuff, and even if we get arrested, he guarantees us a get-out-of-jail-free card. Which I must say is exactly the kind of classy move you'd expect from Arnold. As Larry likes to say: Yes, he's Republican, but not a *real* Republican.

"So are you in or are you in?" Larry says.

I just sigh.

"Babe," he says, "I'm starting to worry about you."

Suddenly I'm overwhelmed by this weird, inexplicable urge to cry. Maybe it's the pot. It makes me weepy sometimes. By the time we hang up there are tears in my eyes. I get up and look at myself in the mirror. It's one of my favorite things to do. I keep mirrors everywhere. I'm looking at myself and thinking, *Jobso, dude, what the hell is wrong with you? Remember who you are, okay, dude? Get a friggin grip.*

I go to the kitchen and call Breezeann, our house manager, at her boyfriend's house and wake her up and have her come over and make me a mango smoothie. Even that doesn't cheer me up. And that *is* scary. Because if a mango smoothie can't cheer me up, I'm definitely in bad shape.

On Sunday night I once again have my most frequent recurring dream—the one in which I'm receiving the Nobel Prize. But this time the dream has a twist. After they give me the prize I find myself out in the street, wearing a loincloth, carrying a cross. People are yelling at me, spitting at me. Then I'm up on the cross, and beside me is Bill Gates, who's also being crucified. "*You* I can see," I say. "But why me?" Gates laughs and says, "You're being crucified because you stole all your best ideas from me."

I wake screaming. It's dawn.

This is my life. You can't believe the stress. It's tough to run any company, but it's an order of magnitude more difficult when you're in a field driven by creativity. My business is all about what's next. We get one product out the door, we need to have five more in the pipeline. And every product is a battle. I used to think the work would get easier as I got older. But if anything the work gets harder. Same goes for all of your creative types. Look at Picasso, or Hemingway. Somebody once asked one of them whether he found it easier to paint or write novels as he got older, since he'd already done so many paintings or novels. I can't remember which one it was, but anyway the answer was no, it was always a struggle. Then Hemingway ended up putting a gun in his mouth, and Picasso died in a bullfight, I think, which is so cool it should be illegal.

Every day I come to work and try to create something magical, and instead I spend all my time putting out fires and fighting this shitstorm of emergencies and distractions, with a million people trying to get in to see me, or hounding me on the phone, and a zillion emails piling up in my inbox. Greenpeace is hounding me because our computers don't turn themselves into compost when you're done with them. Some European Commission is pissed because iTunes and the iPod are designed to work smoothly together. Microsoft, the scourge of the planet, has been chasing me for thirty years, copying everything I do.

On the other hand, I have to admit, in many ways my life is pretty amazing. Thanks to years of exercise and careful attention to dieting, in my early fifties I remain in fantastic physical condition. I am also a talented hypnotist, able to work with individuals in a one-on-one setting or with large groups—like the people who attend Apple press conferences and Macworld shows. The hypnotic power is so powerful that sometimes I have to consciously work on dialing it down. For example, when I walk into the Starbucks on Stevens Creek Boulevard in Cupertino, the girls who work there start flirting with me, and I can tell that they know who I am and they're all nervous, like they're meeting Brad Pitt or Tom Cruise or something. Then their eyes start getting glassy and I know that if I snapped my fingers they would do me right there behind the coffee machine. Or maybe in the restroom, which might be more comfortable and afford us some privacy. Not that I would do that, because I wouldn't. But it's very cool to know that I could.

On the career front, I'm doubly blessed. In addition to running a computer company, I also run a movie studio. Maybe you've heard of it. It's called Disney. Yeah. *That* Disney. Before Disney I ran a movie company called Pixar. We made a few movies that some people have heard of, like *Toy Story* and *Finding Nemo*. I bought Pixar for ten million dollars and sold it to Disney for seven and a half billion. Not a bad return.

Which leads me to my next point. The money issue. For a while I developed a complex about it. But fortunately I'm also a very spiritual person, having devoted many years to the study of Zen Buddhism, and this spirituality has really helped me deal with the guilt. My big breakthrough came on the day when my net worth hit the billion-dollar mark. It's a big deal; ask anyone who's been there. It freaks you out. Because at that point there's no more denying that you're just a regular person. You're not. You're a billionaire.

It's like being in one of those movies where the hero realizes he's got telekinetic powers and it's just too bad if he doesn't want them, he's got them. I remember standing in front of a mirror in my office at Apple, naked, looking at myself. Which is something I do. I check out my body. Once a month I take a photo, and I save them in a digital album that I created in less than a minute using our iPhoto software. Anyway. I'm standing there in front of the mirror on the day that I became a billionaire and I'm going, Steve is a *billionaire*. Steve is a *billionaire*. A *billionaire*. Just saying it over and over, listening to the sound of that word.

The thing about becoming a billionaire is that first you're elated; then you're freaked out; and then you start feeling guilty. But here is where my Zen training helped me. I sat down and meditated and forced myself to not think about my wealth. I was sitting there moaning my syllable, and then I opened my eyes and came out of my trance and I said, out loud, in this really booming voice, to this imaginary critic guy that I imagined was standing there criticizing me for having so much money, I shouted right at him, as loud as I could: "Frig you, ass-munch, because I'm *smarter* than you, I'm *better* than you, I'm *changing the world,* and I *deserve* this."

34

It was this amazing moment of total humility and self-negation. Two days later I woke up and invented the concept for the iPod. True story.

The way I see it, I can't really take credit for being so rich. But it's also not my fault, either. It just is what it is. It's beyond my control. Here's another way to look at it. The other day I was listening to a piece of music. It was a symphony by Mozart, written when he was nine years old. I thought to myself, How the hell does this happen? How does someone like Mozart come to exist? Fair enough, a musical genius spins up out of the gene pool. That probably happens pretty regularly. But in this case the genius happens to land in Salzburg, Austria, in the eighteenth century—the most fertile musical environment that has ever existed. And his father is a music teacher. Boom. Lightning strikes.

Same for me. I was born in San Francisco, in 1955, to a pair of graduate students who put me up for adoption. I landed with a modest couple in a sleepy town called Mountain View, California—which, as luck would have it, was situated right in the heart of what was about to become Silicon Valley. Maybe this was totally random, just natural selection at work. But I wonder if there isn't also some kind of invisible hand of fate moving in our lives. Because imagine that I'd been born in a different century, or in a different place. Imagine I'd been born in some remote village in China. Or imagine that my birth parents didn't put me up for adoption. Imagine my mother kept me, and I grew up in Berkeley with a pair of doofball intellectual parents, and instead of taking a summer job at Hewlett-Packard and meeting Steve Wozniak, I spent my teenage years hanging out in coffee shops reading Sartre and Camus and writing lame-ass poetry.

The point is, my adoption was necessary. It needed to happen. It's like Moses being left in the bullrushes. If that doesn't happen—if Moses stays home with his Jewish mother, and doesn't grow up with Pharaoh's family—well, the Jews don't get out of Egypt, so there's no Ten Commandments, and no Passover, which means no Easter. All of history is changed. Same with me. Without the fluke of my adoption, there's no Apple Computer, no Macintosh, no iMac, no iPod, no iTunes.

I realize how I sound. I sound like a dick. Self-centered. Obnoxious. I'm told all the time that I seem like a narcissistic egomaniac. You know what I say? I say, "Look, wouldn't you be an egomaniac if you woke up one day and found out you were me? You know you would."

Of course the bad part of being such a mega-rich mega-famous mega-creative genius is that there are always some jerks looking to take a shot at you.

In my case those jerks include the United States government, and despite everything I've done for the world—or maybe because of it—they are determined to put me out of business.

Monday morning I arrive at the Jobs Pod, where Ja'Red, my assistant, is looking distressed.

"Dude," he says, "can you make them leave? Like, they're totally polluting the karma."

"Who is?"

"Uh, *them?*" he says, pulling a face and pointing down the hall.

He means Sampson and his lawyers. They've set up camp in the David Crosby conference room. We have five conference rooms in the executive suite—Crosby, Stills, Nash, Young and Dylan—and we had to give them one. I was like, "No way are they using the Dylan room, because Dylan is sacred to me. Put them in Crosby." For one thing, I can't stand David Crosby. More important, the Crosby room is the farthest away from the Jobs Pod.

"I'll see what I can do."

"Totally, man, because it's fucked up, you know? I mean they're like wearing suits and coming down here asking me where's the men's room and do they have to dial nine to get an outside line and I'm like, 'Dude, whatever' you know?"

Ja'Red is barefoot, wearing a Led Zeppelin T-shirt and cargo shorts. He's been my assistant for four months, which I believe is a new record. The main reason he's working out is that he totally worships me. He's been obsessed with Apple all his life. He's read all of the books about me. He even went to Reed College and then dropped out and lived on a commune and went to India, just like I did. The weirdest thing is that he looks like me. Or, rather, like a twenty-five-year-old version of me. He wears his hair cropped short, like mine, and has the same Arafat half-beard, though his isn't gray. He even wears little round glasses like mine, and sometimes he'll sport jeans and black mock turtlenecks and sneakers. The only difference is he's about an inch shorter than I am.

I met him through his girlfriend. She's twenty years old and works behind the smoothie counter at a health food store in Palo Alto and wears a bike helmet indoors, while she works. One day she was kind of flirting with me and then she invited me to come see her dance troupe perform in San Francisco. The show was called a "fable in dance" and it combined *Alice in Wonderland* and *Little Red Riding Hood* but was set in Iraq, and featured a giant George Bush *papier-mache* doll performing unnatural acts with a giant Dick Cheney *papier-mache* doll, set to the music of the White Stripes. The dancing consisted of twelve spastics in bike shorts leaping around as if they had Saint Vitus' dance and shouting about no blood for oil. I hung around for the whole show. I guess I thought I'd get lucky with Bike Helmet Girl. I was smitten. What can I say? It happens to old men. Yes, I was the only one in the audience over thirty years old. Yes, I felt like the dude in *Death in Venice*. I just kept telling myself, at least she's not a boy.

Afterward, Bike Helmet Girl introduced me to Ja'Red. She hadn't said anything about having a boyfriend, but whatever. Turns out he's an extreme Apple fanboy. When I shook his hand, he cried. The next day he showed up at Apple headquarters, barefoot, and said we could either hire him or call the police. Fair enough, I knew what he was up to, because this is how I got my job at Atari back in the seventies. As it happens I had just fired my previous assistant because he wanted to know, when I asked for a chai latte at exactly one hundred and sixty-five degrees, if I meant Fahrenheit or Celsius. Idiot.

So I hired Ja'Red on the spot, right there in the lobby, and made him my personal assistant, with the official title of "Apprentice Wizard at Large." I went with him to the HR department and waited while they did his retina scan, drew his blood for DNA typing, and gave him an ID badge.

Ja'Red said he was so psyched to work here that we wouldn't even have to pay him; in fact he would pay us. But when I asked the HR woman how much we should charge him she said we couldn't do that because it could be considered indentured servitude, which apparently has been outlawed by the fascist Republicans who run this country. In the end we settled on a salary of twelve thousand dollars a year and free food in the Apple cafeterias.

You should have seen him when I took him for his first tour through the headquarters building. He was like, "Duuude. Duuude. I'm, like, in the temple. Oh my God. Duuude. I feel like

I should be kneeling down or something." I have to admit, it is a pretty impressive place. The most striking thing to outsiders is the silence. I think of the headquarters building as a sacred place, a center of contemplation. Lots of natural materials, like heavy wooden beams and rock walls; and sharp angles, clean lines, cantilevered balconies extending out over huge open spaces. I drew my design ideas from Fallingwater, the Frank Lloyd Wright house in Pennsylvania. Only instead of building around an existing stream and waterfall I had to create a stream and a waterfall. The biggest challenge was to create the impression that the boulders and stream had been there all along, and that the building had been set up around them.

The rest of the campus isn't like this, of course. Those are the buildings where people who aren't me work. They're just like regular office buildings. The engineering labs are the worst. They're absolute pigsties. Pizza boxes everywhere, trash cans overflowing. But that's how the engineers like it.

We spent some time riding around the campus on Segways—I bought a thousand of them when they first came out—and going from one building to another, playing with the retina scanners and voice activated greeters. You should have seen Ja'Red crack up the first time the greeter said, "Good morning, Ja'Red." I showed him through our cafeterias, which serve gourmet ethnic food—Japanese, Thai, Indian, Mexican, three kinds of regional Chinese—all cooked by authentic chefs brought in from those countries.

Like everyone who visits us, he was knocked out by the eighty-foot by twenty-foot multi-touch screens that we have installed throughout the campus. People use them as message boards, or just to write down great ideas for wild new products or design concepts. Some people just draw pictures. Whatever. The idea is to let people express their creativity in a public space. And because it's a touch screen we can capture everything that's put on the screen and feed these ideas into a database and sift them and study them using brainiac algorithms.

Finally I brought him upstairs and showed him the executive suite. We started in the conference room. I showed him how the shade of white that I chose for the walls is exactly the right color to set against the particular shade of blue that we get in the sky in northern California. I explained the principles that had informed my design of the room, and how much time I spent working out the size of the windows and the size of the space between the windows so that the ratio would be perfect. I told him how the board had complained and called me selfish when the building went up and the workmen were off by an inch and a half and I insisted that we knock down one side of the building and build it again so that the window-to-wall ratio would work out perfectly.

"I couldn't focus. The balance was off. In the end I was right, and everyone agreed. But like everything else around here, it was a battle. You'll see. It's how the world is. Everyone's ready to compromise. Take my advice. Don't listen to other people. Don't ever settle for ninety-nine-point-nine-nine percent."

Next stop was the meditation room, where we sat on mats and listened to Ravi Shankar, whom Ja'Red had never heard of. Finally I showed him my office. He was trembling when we walked in. I let him sit in my leather chair, which was custom-made for Ludwig Mies van der Rohe. I showed him my private bathroom—I'm unable to go to the bathroom in places used by other people, even at home; it's one of my quirks—and the meeting room and kitchen, which, like the bathroom, I cannot share with anyone. I showed him my workspace, which consists of four thirty-inch Cinema displays set side by side, powered by an eight-core MacPro connected by Gigabit Ethernet to a stack of dedicated Xserve quad-processor blade servers and a ten-terabyte Xserve RAID array.

"Duuude," he said, "I just want to sit here and soak it in."
Then he began to cry. Again.

"Seriously, dude," he says, handing me my messages and a cup of green tea. "Do something, okay? I mean the rest of us have to work here, and we're trying to focus or whatever and these douchebags in suits are just running around giving orders and whatever."

"Okay. Where's Mayzie?"

Mayzie is Ja'Red's assistant. I don't know much about her except that she seems to be about his age and I think he met her through his mountain biking club. She has lots of tattoos and piercings, including a bolt in her bottom lip, which makes it impossible for me to look directly at her. Piercings in general are a huge problem for me, but the facial ones really freak me out.

"Yeah, she's coming in late because, um, like they had to take their dog to the vet for a checkup, and her boyfriend was going to do it, but he like hurt his foot or something in this drum circle last night and so he can't drive or something because they have a stick shift car and it's his left foot, and, um . . ."

He's still explaining when I close the door to the Jobs Pod. I sit down at my main desk, which is made from a single two-inch board hand hewn from the heartwood of a Giant Sequoia and which never, ever, has had anything placed on it. No computer, no phone, no papers, no cups, no pens. All that stuff goes on another desk off at the side of the room. The main desk is only for thinking and praying. I begin every workday with a few minutes of quiet reflection. I'll contemplate a Zen koan, or chant the Heart Sutra, for example.

But Ja'Red is right. There's a disturbance in the force. I do some breathing exercises and try to get clear, but it's no use. The lawyers are messing us up.

I go down the hall to see them. They've turned the Crosby into their own little war room, with a coffee machine and a tray of unhealthy pastries and a gaggle of paralegals and other assistants from Sampson's law firm who are whizzing around with carts full of folders. Sampson's lawyers are sitting around the conference table, slurping coffee and snooping through folders and booting up their Windows PCs. On that point, I'm sorry, but this is utter provocation. That little stupid sound they make when they boot up. And they are *always* rebooting. Dammit! How can anyone work in this building when this poison is wafting through our hallways? Are they trying to make me crazy?

Nevertheless, for sport, I smile and say hello and introduce myself to all of them. I tell them how welcome they are. I ask if they need anything, like maybe some real computers, ha ha, and then I shift into Messiah mode and go to the whiteboard and start telling them about some new products, drawing lots of scientific looking lines and arrows and acronyms.

Meanwhile I'm using all sorts of neuro-linguistic programming trigger words, and within seconds I can see that one of Sampson's team members, a lawyer named Chip, has gone under. His eyes have rolled back up into his head, and the tip of his tongue is sticking out of his mouth. In five minutes I'll have the whole room hypnotized. They'll forget all about these options. I'll have them skipping out of the building and shrieking because they imagine the guy in the UPS truck is Britney Spears jumping out of a limo.

But Charlie Sampson is on to me straight away, and he knows exactly how to break the trance. He claps his hands down on the table. His boy snaps awake. "Steve," Sampson says, "great seeing you. Thanks for visiting."

8

It's Monday, so the rest of the morning is devoted to Pilates and yoga, then a working lunch (miso soup, apple slices) with Lars Aki, our industrial designer. Lars has a Danish mother and a Japanese father, and he grew up in England. He's thirty-five years old and looks like a male model. He's totally lean and ripped, but not muscle-bound. He's also one hundred percent gay, and spends huge amounts of time cruising bath houses and leather bars, picking up trashy dudes and getting arrested for smoking crystal meth. Our PR people are constantly trying to cover up some mess he's created. We all wish he'd settle down and find a nice guy and maybe adopt some Chinese kids or something. But what can we do? He's universally recognized as the world's most talented industrial designer.

We're meeting to discuss his proposal to reduce the length of the next iPod by half a millimeter. I think losing half a millimeter throws off the balance of the design, and suggest a quarter of a millimeter instead. As usual, Lars is blown away by the way I take his idea and improve on it.

"You know," he says, "I may have been first in my class at the Royal Academy, but I am always amazed by how much better you are at design than I am. Amazing."

Next we go over some iPhone FPPs (Fake Product Prototypes) that we'll be distributing around Apple and to some of our suppliers to keep people confused about what the actual product is going to look like. Even with our fake products I insist on the highest standards and so I give him my usual critique: "These are total shit," I say.

He just shrugs and gives me his usual weary smile, the one that says, "Steve, you're the toughest boss I've ever had, but I love you because you push me to bring out the best in myself. And if I ever find you asleep and there's no one around, I am going to kill you."

We finish up with twenty minutes of hanging upside down in gravity boots, doing some brainstorming. No big ideas emerge.

I have the afternoon blocked off for Ross Ziehm, our PR guy. Ross is the ultimate flack, a cross between a pit bull and a weasel, but with the face of a schoolboy. He began his career at IBM, then moved on to the National Rifle Association. After that he worked for Pacific Gas & Electric during the years when they were being sued by Erin Brockovich for putting chemicals into groundwater that caused cancer. His spin on that? "First, the science was flawed. Second, nobody forced these people to live in this town and drink the water." Talk about balls. Nothing fazes this guy. He's perfect.

The great thing about Ross is that although he has a heart of pure evil, on the outside he looks like the nicest guy you'd ever meet. Soft-spoken, never swears, uses words like "gosh." He grew up in Long Beach, and is a total Southern California surfer kid. He's in his forties now but he still surfs, down at Maverick's in Santa Cruz, and he's still got the look—tousled blonde hair, whitened teeth, tall and lean, good-looking in that tanned movie-star kind of way. Drives an old beat-up Subaru Outback wagon with his board on the roof and his wetsuit in the back and loads of leftie bumper stickers.

Ross's take on how to handle the Sonya Bourne resignation is to pretend it didn't happen. No announcement, no press release.

"Who pays attention to the general counsel? Just bury it in some SEC filing at the end of the year," he says.

He shows me the draft of the press release we're going to put out announcing that we've brought in a team of lawyers to conduct our internal investigation. I do what I always do. Without even looking at the paper I say, "This is shit. Too wordy. Fourth sentence makes no sense. Transitions need work. Do it again and bring it back."

I make him do his rewrites at a desk outside the Jobs Pod, so I can watch him through the glass wall and bombard him with suggestions via iChat and email. Makes him nuts, but that's how people get creative. You've got to get them a little bit crazy. After five drafts over three hours I sit back in my chair and read the whole thing, very slowly. Then roll it up into a ball and tell him I liked the first one best, so go with that.

He laughs his ass off and says, "Oh, Steve, you know what? I love you, man! What a process! I can't believe it!"

We call the management team together and hand out copies for everyone to review. Ross gives everyone the usual speech about how all press inquiries should be routed to him. He also explains our timing. We're going to put the news out on Thursday, right before the Fourth of July holiday weekend.

"We'll wait until the end of the day West Coast time, after the markets have closed," he says. "The papers back East will have a couple of hours to close their stories before their deadline hits, and their editions will mostly be locked up by then, but I'm sure they'll be able to get some kind of brief item into the paper."

I thank Ross for his excellent presentation and then explain to the team that the really insanely great thing about doing it this way is that people will have all day Friday, the first day of the long Fourth of July holiday weekend, to digest the news, and since the holiday isn't until Tuesday, they'll have at least four more days to mull over this important information. A lot of people will be taking all of next week off, so when they're on the beach with their kids they'll definitely be able to give this story their full attention, and by the time people come back from their break, nearly two weeks from now, they'll know that we here at Apple are really serious about this, um, thing with options or whatever that happened a while ago and we said we are looking into it.

"Steve," says Pete Fisher, our senior vice president of worldwide product marketing, "once again I bow to your genius. What can I say? You're brilliant. Brilliant."

Jim Bell, our COO, says he couldn't agree more. Same with Paul Doezen and Lars Aki. Stephane Villalobos, our head of sales, says he's not a native English speaker but he'd still like to compliment me on how well-written the press release is. Ross Ziehm pipes up to say that he concurs, that I absolutely have a gift for language, which is especially amazing because I'm also such a hardcore electronics genius.

"You could have been one of the great ones," Ross says. "Tolstoy, Steinbeck, Hemingway. Heck, you still could, whenever you decide to write the great American novel."

"Okay," I say, "great meeting. Great feedback. Thanks for your honesty. Really valuable."

By the time we're done it's past six and most people are heading home. But my day is just beginning. I'm off to the Tassajara meditation room with the iPhone circuit board again. Yes, I'm still obsessing about this board. But this product is more important than anything we've ever made. Right now we are living in the middle of what people in the Valley call an extreme inflection point. Every kind of information is going digital. Phone calls, movies, TV shows, music, books. To produce and consume digital media, you need computers. Which means everything around you becomes a computer. Your phone, your TV, your stereo.

Who better to rule this new world than me? Everything I've done during my entire life has been in preparation for this. The past thirty years at Apple were like Act One in a play. Now we are beginning Act Two. Today we are doing twenty billion a year in sales and we have an eighty-billion-dollar market value. Which is great. But it's nothing compared to where we can be in ten years.

Which is why I'm here on a Monday night, trying to perfect this circuit board. What am I searching for? It's hard to put it into words. The thing is, anyone can make a phone, just like anyone can make a computer. But that's not good enough for Apple. Part of what makes us different—and, yes, better—is the way we create products. For example, we don't start with the product itself. We start with the ads. We'll spend months on advertisements alone. This is the reverse of how most companies do it. Everybody else starts with the product, and only when it's done do they go, "Oh, wait, we need some ads, don't we?" Which is why most advertising sucks, because it's an after-thought. Not here. At Apple, advertising is a prethought. If we can't come up with a good ad, we probably won't do the product.

Once we've got the ad campaign, then we start work on the product. But we don't start with the technology. We start with design. Again, different. Lars Aki will bring me fifteen iPhone prototypes. I take them into my meditation room and I go into a trance. Here's the key part: *I don't think about them.* I don't think about anything. Not so easy to do, to think about nothing. But after years of practice I can empty my head and get into this non-thinking state in just a few minutes.

I'll sit for hours, non-thinking about the fifteen prototypes. Gradually, very gradually, one will begin to emerge from the others as the best of the bunch. When that happens I'm done. I'll send the emergent design, as we call it, back to Lars Aki and tell him to start all over, making a hundred or so new prototypes that branch off from this one. From those his team will winnow down the pool to another batch of fifteen winners. I return to the meditation room once again and empty my mind and choose the next emergent design. This process can go on for months, with round after round of emergent designs, and it's all based on non-thinking, intuitive interpretation.

When we finally settle on a physical prototype, we start working on chips and software. We make our own special chips, our own special software. We put the chips and software into the physical design and I do some more non-thinking meditation. Unfortunately it often occurs that the software is amazing but it doesn't feel right in this physical package, and so we have to go back and redesign the phone all over again, employing the same emergent design process. Then there's the color issue. You can't imagine how many shades of black there are. And white. Then we have to consider finishes. Satin, matte, glossy, high-gloss. I'll spend weeks working eighteen-hour days looking at color chips and be drained at the end of each day.

Then there's packaging. We put as much thought, maybe more, into the packaging of the product as we do into the product itself. What we're looking to achieve is this magical sequence that takes place when you open the box. How does the box open? Is there a tongue? Two side slots? What color is the box? Which grade of cardboard do we use? How does it feel to your fingers? And what about inside? Does the iPhone lie flat? Is it tilted up? Is there plastic over it? Do we put a sticky thing over the screen that you have to peel off?

With the iPhone, we'd got all the way through all of these processes. Everything was done. We were ready to ship. But one day I was visiting the hardware lab and I happened to see a circuit board lying out on a workbench. I said, "You're kidding, right? That's not the actual board, is it?"

So I returned to the meditation room. It's maddening for the team. I get a huge amount of grief from the engineers. But this is how I do things. This is my process. And this is why Apple products are special. If you want something non-special, you can buy a Dell.

Mike Dinsmore is the VP of engineering in charge of the iPhone project. He's also a flat-out genius and a huge legend in the Valley, a former professor at UC Berkeley who once won a Turing Award, which for geeks is on a par with the Nobel Prize. He not only developed a version of UNIX but he also designed one of the first RISC microprocessors. He's also a freak of nature: six-foot-five, a big bright shock of Bozo-red hair, Howdy Doody freckles and skin so white he appears fluorescent. And he has absolutely no regard for personal appearance or personal hygiene. If I hadn't hired him ten years ago he'd still be stuck in some lab at Berkeley building tinker toys and living in some crap apartment in Oakland and scaring the bejesus out of girls from the local escort services. Instead, thanks to me, he's a millionaire many times over, living in Atherton with an incredibly hot wife who has enough class not to cheat on him openly and a pack of little fish-pale red-haired kids who are every bit as glow-in-the-dark scary as he is.

He's waiting for me outside the development lab when I arrive on Tuesday to announce the huge breakthrough I've had.

He's wearing black shorts, a black T-shirt and huge black sunglasses. I can't tell if he dresses this way in order to look even more freaky or if he actually believes black clothes look good next to super-pale skin. He's here to escort me into the building. Believe it or not, even though I am Dictator for Life here, there are some buildings that even I am not authorized to enter alone, and this is one of them.

"Welcome," he says, injecting just enough irony into his voice to let me know he doesn't really mean it, because honestly, I'm never welcome in the engineering labs. All I ever do is cause trouble for these guys.

The iPhone team works in a cement-block bunker with no windows and a lead-lined roof to prevent companies from spying on us from airplanes. The hallways are designed like a maze, which deflects sound waves and makes it more difficult for someone to eavesdrop electronically from outside. The whole place gets swept for bugs once a week.

There are only two doors into the building and both have bag scanners and metal detectors, just like at the airport, and they're manned by former Israeli commandos. We go inside and pass through the retina scanner and then into the security foyer. The Israelis glare at us and say nothing.

The iPhone is so secret that we refer to the project only by its code name, Guatama. We don't use the word "phone" or "iPhone" in email or in conversation. To make things even more secure, three-quarters of our engineers aren't even working on the actual iPhone. They're working on FPPs. Even the engineers themselves don't know if they're working on real products or fake ones.

Mike leads me through the concrete maze to the building's conference room. His engineers are in there gobbling pastries and slurping coffee, waiting for us and looking pissed off.

"Namaste," I say to the engineering dorks, bowing slightly

from the waist with my hands pressed together, pretending that I have great respect for their big math-loving brains. "I honor the Buddha inside you."

They grumble and grunt. A couple of them do the "namaste" thing back to me. I'm pretty sure they're taking the piss out of me. One thing I'd forgotten to mention: engineers are the world's biggest assholes.

"So I pulled half of an all-nighter last night," I tell them, "and I've come up with some ideas on the circuit board. We're going to need a complete redesign."

Groans all around, and Mike says, "Steve, before we get into the design review, I'd just like to say that we all have huge amounts of respect for your genius, but the board is designed the way it is because that's the best way to move the signals through the circuit. It's an optimized design. You can't just change it because you don't like the way it looks."

I remind him that, first of all, I can do anything I want, and second, I know they want to kill me but they have to admit that I know how to design products, and I'm sorry but this circuit board for the iPhone is way too ugly.

"There's no balance," I say. "You've got this long piece on the left—"

"That's a memory chip," one of the engineers says, interrupting me.

"And you've got nothing on the right side to balance it out. And the big chip—"

"That's the microprocessor," the smart-ass says, interrupting me again.

I stop and look at him. He's a fat guy with a ponytail and a little soul-patch juice-mop beard and a Dead Kennedys T-shirt.

"The *big chip*," I say, "should be right in the middle, not off-center. The two little gold pieces on the right should be lined up straight. You've got all these little skinny lines on one side then big fat lines on the other, with loads of space. Come on, guys. Go back and redo this. I want it perfectly symmetrical."

Mike says if we arrange the chips the way I'm suggesting, the circuit won't work. "We'll get signal bleed," he says.

"Just try it," I say. "Do it and let's see."

The know-it-all guy says, "With all due respect, we're electrical engineers, okay? I think we might have a little insight into what we're doing."

He gets up out of his chair and goes to the whiteboard and starts trying to give me a lesson in how electric current flows through a circuit. I know he thinks he's being the big hero, standing up to the tyrant boss. What he doesn't notice is that all of the other guys are staring down at their hands, like a little herd of sheep averting their eyes when one of their fellow sheep is about to be picked off by a wolf.

I press my hands together in my prayer position. I go all very weird and quiet. When he's done with his lecture, I say, in the softest voice I can produce, "Excuse me, but what is your name?"

"Jeff," he says.

"Jeff. Good. Jeff, please put down that marker and leave the building. Drop your badge at the security checkpoint. Mike will process your paperwork this afternoon."

"What? I'm fired?"

"You know," I say, "you pick things up fast. You must be an engineer, right?"

Later in the day Mike Dinsmore comes to see me and tells me Jeff didn't mean to be rude but he's having a tough time at home, his wife has some terminal illness and they've got three kids and one of them is in a wheelchair and needs a special van, blah blah blah.

"Oh," I say, "I had no idea."

He stands there. I let him wait.

Finally he says, "So?"

I go, "Mike, who's your supervisor?"

"Ted Reibstein."

"Okay. Hold on."

I press my speakerphone and buzz Ja'Red and tell him to get Ted Reibstein from engineering on the phone.

When Ted picks up I say, "Ted, this is Steve. I'm here with Mike Dinsmore. I'm sending him down to your office so you can fire him and process his paperwork. And there's a guy who works for him, Jeff something, who also needs to be fired. Mike will explain."

"Sure thing," Ted says.

Mike stands there with his jaw hanging open. I spin around in my chair, facing away from him, and start checking my email. When I turn back he's still standing there, towering over my desk like some freako red-haired giant from *Lord of the Rings*, clenching and unclenching his fists.

I call Ja'Red again and tell him to have security send up Avi and Yuri. "Tell them to bring their Tasers," I say. That sends the big freak running.

I'm often asked about my management style, especially since I gave that amazing commencement speech at Stanford and everyone realized what an incredibly deep thinker I am. I've seen those Internet rumors about how I didn't really write that speech, how I hired some ghostwriter. All I can say is: Please. The guy fixed some grammar errors and punched it up a bit. But I'm the one who spent half a day in Longs Drug Store reading Hallmark cards to gather material.

Like everything else at Apple, my management approach is a little bit different. I never subscribed to the conventional wisdom of the East Coast management experts like Jack Welch. For example, Welch says do a lot of reviews and always let people know where they stand. I say, No way. In fact, quite the opposite. *Never let people know where they stand.* Keep them guessing. Keep them afraid. Otherwise they get complacent. Creativity springs from fear. Think of a painter, or a writer, or a composer working furiously in his studio, afraid he's going to starve to death if he doesn't get his work done. That's where greatness comes from. Same goes for the people at Apple and Pixar. They come in every day knowing it could be their last day. They work like hell; trust me.

Because you know what? *Fear works.* Look at the crappy cars that get made in Detroit, where nobody ever gets fired. Compare that to the stuff that gets made in Vietnamese sweatshops. Or to the bridge in *The Bridge on the River Kwai*. Please don't say that bridge was awesome because the Brits were such amazing perfectionists. Come on. I love the Brits, but these are not people who are known for the quality of their workmanship. Ever owned a Jaguar? Enough said. No, what motivated those lazy, stupid Brits was their fear of the efficient, vicious Japanese. You put people's lives in danger, and they do their best work.

Obviously we can't *literally* put our employees' lives at risk. But we have to make them feel that way. This requires a lot of psychological manipulation on our part. But look at the result. We never could have made OS X so reliable if our engineers didn't believe in their hearts that every time a bug surfaced one man was going to be killed.

Which leads me to my next management tip. *You don't have to hire the best people.* You can hire anyone, as long as you scare the shit out of them. That's the key. The fear. This applies not only to assembly line and factory workers but to all of your staff, including top executives and even the board of directors. A corollary to this rule is this: *Only promote stupid people.* But not just any stupid people. You have to find the certain type of stupid people who actually believe they're super brilliant. They make insanely great managers and are incredibly easy to manipulate. It's easy to spot them. Former McKinsey consultants are top candidates.

The MBAs say you should set high standards, let people know what's expected of them, and hold them to that. I do a little twist on that and say, Hold people to an *impossibly* high standard, but here's the twist—*don't tell them what that standard is.* And fire them if they fall short. You know what that does to people? Makes them crazy. And guess what? Crazy people are more creative. And more productive. Every shrink in the world knows this.

Another MBA rule that I never follow is where they say a CEO or manager should be consistent and predictable. I say the opposite. *Be inconsistent and unpredictable.* Be random. One day say something is great and the guy who made it is a genius. The next day say it's crap, and he's a moron. Watch how hard that guy will work now, trying to impress you.

Management gurus also tell you to reward performance, and dole out loads of praise. I disagree. My motto is this: *No praise. Ever.* You start praising people and pretty soon they start thinking they're as smart as you are. You cannot have this. All employees must know at all times that you are better in every way than they are. Repeated criticism, in the most humiliating fashion, is one way to accomplish this.

The best way to keep people's spirits broken is *to fire people on a regular basis for no reason.* Fly off the handle, shout at people, call them names, then fire them. Or better yet, don't fire them. Let them believe they survived for a few days. Then, when they're relaxed, call them in and fire them. It's all part of creating and maintaining the culture of fear.

Another tactic, but one that should only be used in extreme circumstances, is this: *throw tantrums.* I mean literally cry and scream and roll around on the floor like a three-year-old, slapping your hands and kicking your feet. This is great when someone won't let you have your way. It works because it freaks people out to see a grown man crying and screaming. They'll do anything to make it stop. Brilliant.

Another tactic involves a verbal technique based on neurolinguistic programming. In the middle of a meeting, when someone else is talking, I'll sit there nodding my head, as if I'm agreeing with everything they say. But then at some point I'll suddenly stand up and go, "No! No! That's stupid! What is *wrong* with you? Did someone drop you on your head when you were a baby? I can't fucking *believe* this!" Then I'll stomp out of the room, slamming the door.

Another trick is I'll get on the elevator with some Apple employees, and smile, or say hi. They're usually nervous, and usually they're so scared that they just don't talk at all, and I have to admit, I dig that. But sometimes they do carry on a conversation with each other, one that does not include me. When that happens I'll wait until we get to my floor, and then, as the door opens, I'll turn and say, "What you just said is completely wrong. You know not whereof you speak. Please go clean out your desk, and turn in your badge at the HR department."

This freaks people out, believe me.

I've described these management techniques in presentations at business schools, and I always get the same blowback. People go on and on, telling me that using fear and psychological manipulation doesn't work. They say it works better to be nice to people and treat them with respect. Last time this happened was at Stanford and the guy giving me grief was the professor. Perfect. I hate professors. I was like, "Look at Apple. Look at our amazing success. Especially our success since I took over the company. Compare that to the abject failure under my predecessors. Now compare that to whatever company that you built with your bare hands into a multi-billion-dollar empire using your techniques. What's that? You don't have a company? You never started a company or ran a company? You've never been a CEO? Huh. Okay. So you're, what, a teacher? In a college or something? Okay. The prosecution rests."

It's dawn on the Fourth of July. I'm in my backyard, facing the back wall and the flower garden. During the night a low fog has rolled in over the hills from the Pacific. I'm standing in the foggy mist, wearing shorts and an old Reed College T-shirt. I'm facing east. For a long time I am absolutely still. I listen to my breathing. I feel my heart beating, the pulse in my neck and wrists and ankles. Slowly, I raise my arms over my head and begin my sun salutation sequence. From this I shift into my T'ai Chi workout, focusing on my breath energy, which is incredible this morning, really off the meter.

It's been a crazy weekend. On Friday the story hit the papers about our announcement that we have hired lawyers to investigate ourselves. Since then, every day, there have been more stories, all of them based on leaks and "sources close to the matter." I've been back and forth on the phone with Ross Ziehm and Tom

Bowditch and Moshe Hishkill, our head of security, trying to find out who's talking to the press. We're pulling phone logs, scanning emails, but so far we can't find anything.

But that's behind us. Today there is peace. I can feel it. Today I refuse to read any newspapers or watch the news on TV. Today I will only focus on restoring my strength. By eight in the morning I've finished my workout, showered, and downed a fruit smoothie that Breezeann prepared for me. Breezeann is a true flower child California chick, raised by hippie parents in the Santa Cruz mountains, in a cabin with no running water or electricity. The only question I asked her during her job interview was how many times she had taken acid. "Oh, man," she said, "I dunno, but, like, a lot? Like I couldn't even count even?" The only question she had for us was, "Um, like, I wouldn't have to wear like business type clothing or anything, right?"

In other words: perfect. She also happens to have long blonde hair and a killer body and she bears a strong resemblance to the naked chick on the cover of the "Blind Faith" album. I think about her every morning when I'm beating off in the shower, and I've been wanting to bone her forever. But every time I ask her to sleep with me she threatens to rat me out to Mrs. Jobs, and I have to give her a raise. She's now making two hundred and fifty thousand dollars a year. I don't know what we'd do without her.

"Namaste," I tell her as I'm leaving. I do a little bow. "I honor the place where you and I are one."

"Yeah," she says, without looking up from washing the blender in the sink. "Keep dreaming, sport."

Then it's off to Apple headquarters for my weekly high colonic. Yes, it's a holiday, and yes, my colonic tech, Kuso Suka-toro, isn't exactly psyched about coming to work. So much for that famous Japanese work ethic.

"You clenching," Kuso says. "Not good. You need relax."

We work on it, and eventually I'm fully refreshed. Right after the butt blast I ride a Segway down to the back of the campus to the commando barracks. Moshe Hishkill is waiting for me. Moshe is a former general in the Israeli army. He's got this huge scar, as wide as a finger, down the left side of his face, and a messed-up left eye that looks like egg yolk. We've left medical catalogs on his desk, open to the page with eyepatches; he doesn't seem to get the hint.

Moshe introduces me to a guy named Mikhail, one of the Russian hackers from our Windows Virus Creation Team (WVCT). "Operation Wavecat," as we call it, employs some of the best virus writers in the world, who do nothing but create malware to mess up Windows computers. I figure if Microsoft really wants to keep copying everything we do and stealing all of our ideas, the least we can do is repay the favor by making their knock-offs not work right.

But right now Mikhail is working on a different project. He's trying to find our leaker. He's a tall guy, dark-haired, with a few days growth of beard. He looks like he hasn't slept for a while.

"I've checked the Apple email and phone system," he says. "Is nothing there. Then, I check—"

He stops and looks at Moshe. He's worried, I guess, about how much he should say in front of me.

"It's okay," I say.

Moshe nods.

He goes on. "I check email addresses that have sent or received anything with Apple email address. Nothing. I check home phones of Apple employees. I check personal email addresses, if we know them. I check cell phones. Is not one hundred percent. But anyway, I get nothing."

"Yeah. That's what I figured. Worth a try, though. Thanks."

I start to leave.

Moshe says, "Wait. There is something."

"Only a clue," Mikhail says. "We have database of phone numbers and email addresses for reporters, Wall Street analysts, business partners, suppliers, customers. I pull information for any reporters who write stories this past weekend. Look. This one. Here. Girl from *Wall Street Journal*."

He pulls up a page on his screen. It's an AT&T phone bill for Erika Murphy, a *Journal* reporter in San Francisco. He scrolls through the list of her incoming and outgoing calls over the past two months.

"This one," he says, stopping on a line. "Here. And here again. And here, an incoming call. Here, an outgoing call. A dozen calls with same number. So I pull up some other reporters. Same number calls three other people."

"That's not an Apple number."

"No, certainly not."

"What is it? A cell phone?"

"A SIM card. But we can tell where it was used."

"How do you do that? Satellites or something?"

"Don't ask," Moshe says.

"It's a weird thing." Mikhail turns from his screen and looks at me. "You know anyone in the Cayman Islands?"

By the time I get home Larry has already arrived.

"It's definitely weird," he says, when I tell him about the phone calls from the Cayman Islands.

"No talking about work," Mrs. Jobs says. "Just for tonight. Okay?"

"What else are we supposed to talk about?"

"I don't know. How about books," she says.

We look at her.

"Movies? Politics? The war in Iraq?"

We sit there for a couple of minutes, stymied. Finally Mrs. Jobs goes into the house to get a drink and Larry says, "Did you hear about Jeff Fernandez? He's selling his house. Legal bills. He's going to be ruined."

"Jesus."

"Yup. It's bad, brother."

Breezeann fires up the grill and cooks up some mind-blowing tofu steaks and grilled veggies. After dinner we walk to the park to watch the fireworks. We all go "ooh" and "aah" at the right moments, and we walk home saying how great the show was this year and pretending that everything is going to be okay.

13

On the day after the holiday I arrive at work to find a hand-written note from Charlie Sampson informing me that he and his team would like me to come down and answer some questions. At the appointed hour I go to the Crosby room. They're all lined up behind a long table. They have a stenographer, some recording equipment, and pitchers of water.

"Dudes," I say, "what's this? The Senate subcommittee?"

Nobody laughs.

"Seriously," I say, "this looks pretty intense. Should I have a lawyer or something?"

"Do you think you need a lawyer?" Sampson says.

"That's what I just asked you."

"I think you should do what you think is best. If you feel like you can't answer our questions without having a lawyer present, then you should get a lawyer. But this isn't a court. We're not here to decide if you're guilty of anything."

"All right," I say. "Fire away."

Sampson starts out asking some time-wasting stuff like my name and how old I am and how long I've worked at the company. For kicks I get a couple of them wrong, just to see if they're paying attention. They are.

Sampson asks me what percentage of Apple's outstanding shares I own. I tell him I have no idea.

"None at all? You mean you could own one percent or ninety percent, and you really don't know?"

"I've told you this already. I'm no good with numbers. It's part of the reason I left school. It's a learning disability. I'm mathlexic."

"Mathlexic?"

"It's like being dyslexic, only with numbers."

Sampson frowns. "This is a real diagnosis?"

"It's either mathlexic or dysmathic. I can't remember. One or the other."

"Are you also dyslexic?"

I shake my head. "Just dysmathic."

"I thought it was mathlexic," one of the young guys says, in this *gotcha* voice.

"Oooh," I say, "you caught me! Look, you Nazis, I told you I'm not sure what it's called. And watch your tone, assholes. I'm the one signing your paychecks, remember?"

"That's actually not true," one of them says.

Sampson says we should move on. His helpers start firing questions at me. Normally in situations like this I can pretty much read people's minds. It's a form of extrasensory perception that I developed by working with a Zen master in Los Altos. On a really good day it's almost like hearing a transcript of what someone is thinking. But today I'm getting static. Images, flashes. Stray words and phrases. Random stuff.

When I look at Sampson I get nothing at all. He stares back at me and does something funky with his eyes.

The helper named Chip says, "Do you recall a lunch meeting with Sonya Bourne on the thirteenth of July in 2001 at which you two discussed options grants?"

"Let me see," I say. "2001? Thirteenth of July?" I close my eyes and wait a few seconds, as if I'm concentrating. "Ah, right. Okay. Yes. July 13, 2001. It was a Tuesday. We went to Il Fornaio in Palo Alto. I had a Waldorf salad and a bottle of San Pellegrino. I sent the salad back because there was mayonnaise in the dressing and had them make it again with a vinaigrette dressing, and the waiter said then it won't be a Waldorf salad and I said that's fine, bring me what I want. Waiter's name was Anton. Six-one, slender, brown curly hair. Wore a silver ring on his right hand, middle finger. Timex sport watch on his left wrist. Sonya had a turkey club sandwich, no bacon, light mayo, and a Diet Coke with a wedge of lemon. No, strike that. Wedge of lime. The bill came to twenty-three dollars and nineteen cents. I left a two-dollar tip. Paid with a Visa card."

Chip scowls. "So that's a no?"

"Do you remember where you were on some random day five years ago? Come on."

They start going on about how many options I received on what day and how many I exercised and how many I sold, and then how many I gave back in exchange for restricted shares, and what's the value of those shares today versus when I got them, and wasn't some of that money applied to the value of the jet that Apple gave me, and then they start going on about some Black-Scholes model or whatever to figure out the value of the compensation.

"Guys," I say, "seriously, I have no idea what you're talking about. It's like you're not speaking English."

"Let's try going over this again," Sampson says.

"You can go over it all you want," I say, "but I won't understand a word. I told you, I'm dysmathic."

"That's going to be your defense?" Sampson says. "Seriously?"

"What can I tell you. It's a disability." I stand up. "Are we done?"

"No," Sampson says. "Not even close."

"Well," I say, "I'm done. You guys can stay if you want."

"**There's something** you need to see," Paul Doezen says.

He's waiting for me outside my office. He's a mountain of a man, Buddha in a suit, grunting as he hoists himself up out of his chair.

He hands me a piece of paper. The paper contains rows and columns of numbers. It's a spreadsheet. I detest spreadsheets. I refuse to read them.

"Just tell me what this means," I say.

Paul explains that the key numbers are the ones in the right-hand column. They represent the number of Apple shares that are currently sold short in the market, meaning the number of shares held by frigtards who are betting that our stock is going to go down. The number, Paul says, has been growing steadily over the past month, starting right before the SEC hassle began.

"Notice I said *before* the SEC thing happened. What's that all about, right? Someone knew there was bad news coming. And since then someone's been shorting us like crazy. There's a big spike right here. You see? And look at the daily volume. Then look at the ratio of shorts to daily trading volume, and the ratio of shorts to overall float. Look at the churn."

I have no idea what he's talking about.

"Someone's making a bet against us," he says. "A big bet. And it looks like they're trying to cover it up so we won't notice it. The key is in the number of shares that get traded every day. That number for us has gone up by a huge amount all of a sudden, for no apparent reason. At the same time the number of shares sold short has gone way up too. It's weird. I'm not sure if they're connected. But they might be."

He looks at me.

"Do you understand this?"

"Do I look like I understand this? I have no idea why you're even telling me this. Do you realize in the time we've spent having this conversation I could have developed a new feature for the next iPod? Too late, though, because now it's gone. The idea has flown away. Are you happy now?"

"The thing you should be aware of," he says, "is what might happen next. The short sellers are betting that the stock is going to go down. If, instead, it goes up, they get killed. They lose money."

"I know what short-selling is."

"So okay. You get a bunch of these asshole shorts piling into your stock, they tend to get impatient for the stock to go down. So they tend to start spreading rumors to knock the price down. You might want to tell the PR guys to be ready for it."

"That's it? That's why you're here taking up my time? So you can tell me that I should tell the PR guys that someone might start spreading rumors?"

"It's my job to keep the CEO informed. As the CFO, I have a fiduciary responsibility—"

"Okay, spare me. Now I've got a better idea. *You* go tell the PR guys about this, and let me get back to being creative. You also might want to find out who's actually behind all the short selling. Have you thought of that?"

"Probably some hedge fund. I've put out some calls. So far nobody knows. Kind of weird. I'll stay on it."

15

So Bono is in town, because now in addition to being a rock star he's also got this investment company with a bunch of Silicon Valley private equity scumbags, who are even worse than venture capitalists, if that's actually possible. They've told him they'll double his money in five years, which in Valley speak means they are going to fleece him for every penny he's stupid enough to give them. So far he's forked over twenty million. I don't have the heart to tell him the truth. He's having so much fun.

Plus it's hilarious to hear him talk about deals as if he actually knows something about technology. Like one time we were talking and he said something about "speeds and feeds," and I asked him, "Excuse me, but did you say 'speeds and feeds'? Do you even know what that means?" Of course he had no idea. But you know what? He's no worse than all the other bozos who come out here with their MBAs and no background in tech and after six months they've picked up the lingo and suddenly they're believing they're going to spot the next Google and get rich.

Thing is, I should hate Bono, if only because he stole my shtick—false modesty and lots of noise about wanting to make the world a better place—and took it to a whole new level. Now he's a perennial candidate for the Nobel Prize, while I'm getting savaged by the European Union for being some big ugly American cultural imperialist shitbag capitalist. But give Bono credit. He figured something out that I didn't. One word: Africa. The place is like a miracle worker shrine, a whole continent filled with absolution. Touch it, and you're healed. No matter who you are, no matter how greedy or rotten, if you invoke the cause of helping Africans you get a free pass on everything else. Sure, Bono didn't think this up himself. He stole it from Princess Diana. Now Bill Gates has jumped on the Africa bandwagon too. And Madonna.

But whatever. I like Bono. He's the only person I know who's more self-absorbed than I am. Which, when you're not feeling good about your life, can be a really great thing. With Bono you can hang out all night and never once get to talk about your problems. You just listen to Bono blather on about AIDS and Africa and poverty and debt relief and how The Edge still can't tune his friggin guitar by ear, even after all these years, and he still needs to use one of those electronic tuners instead. Oh, believe me, Bono is the black hole of Calcutta when it comes to conversation. A real barrel of laughs. If you ever start thinking your life sucks, spend some time listening to Bono and his sob stories.

So we started out in this bar in Palo Alto, and he gets hammered, of course. Next thing I know he's sobbing. Says he's seen this stupid Al Gore movie about global warming and he's freaking out.

"Oh, Steve," he says, "you should see the poor polar bears. *Drownin!* We gotta do sumfin, like have a concert or whatever."

So I tell him, hey, first of all, a real polar bear would bite your friggin head clean off and eat you alive. "They're not exactly these cuddly little animal friends that Al Gore probably told you they are."

Second, I told him, "You know, not to sound condescending or whatever, because definitely I'd like to go plan a little charity concert with you, but I'm pretty busy these days, because in case you haven't been reading the papers lately, the feds are trying to put me in jail. Meanwhile I'm trying to develop a new phone, and a new TV device, and I'm working on a presentation for our big developers conference which is only a month away, and I'm also putting the finishing touches on a new video iPod that holds four and a half hours of full motion video, which means one day soon we are going to wake up in a world where you can carry two full-length movies in your pocket. Think about that. Boom. Game over."

Mr. Bono the Rock Star says, "Jaysus! Another fookin iPod? You're like Willy fookin Wonka in his fookin chocolate factory, out there baking up your fookin iPods, and meanwhile the fookin planet is fookin meltin, ya fooktard."

I tell him, "Bono, look, we all gotta do what we do, right? You wouldn't call up Picasso and ask him to stop painting so he could work on global warming, would you? You wouldn't call up Gandhi or Martin Luther King or Nelson Mandela and say, 'Hey, put aside that human rights stuff and come save some penguins on the Greenland ice cap,' right?"

Bono says there are no penguins on the Greenland ice cap, they're all down on the South Pole or whatever, like he's Mr. Ecology Expert now that he snoozed through some movie. As far as I know the guy didn't even finish high school. Then he starts calling me an *eejit* and telling me I should be putting all of Apple's profits into some fund to save the planet.

I do what I always do when I want to drive someone nuts: I go Zen on him. I get all calm, and I say, "Riiiight, grasshopper, let me run that one past the board of directors. Give away all of our profits. We'll put that on the top of the agenda for our next meeting." Then I go, "Hey man, I'm going into a tunnel, man, oh shit, can you hear me? Zzzzzzh. Zzzzzzzzh."

Apparently he's not as drunk as I thought because he says, "Cocknose, I'm sitting right here next to you at a table, remember? We're not even on a fookin phone."

"Oh, what? Mmmmm . . . can't hear . . . zzzhhhzzhh . . . what? You there? Can you hear me? Zhhhzhhh . . . Hey I'll call you back, okay?"

"Seriously, Steve."

"Seriously, Bono. Look, I'm telling you this 'cause I'm your friend. You need to get a grip, dude."

So we pay our tab—let me clarify; *I* pay our tab, because in case you didn't know this, Bono is probably the cheapest person in the entire world, and he never carries money, saying it's because Jesus never carried money, but really it's so he never has to pay for anything—and we drive up to the city. Bono insists he's okay to drive, and maybe it's an Irish thing or something because, even though he could barely walk out to the car, once he's behind the wheel he's fine, even when I'm passing him a joint and he needs to take his eyes off the road for a second to grab it.

We spend way too much money on dinner at some incredibly overpriced restaurant where the waiters cop all sorts of huge 'tude when I order raw vegetables and insist on having the vegetables presented to me before they're prepared and served. During dinner I try to tell Bono about the trouble I'm in with the SEC, but he won't even pay attention.

"Come on," he says, "let's go hit the Mitchell Brothers." He goes there every time he's in town and runs straight to the room where you sit in the dark on couches and everybody gets a flashlight and you watch some chick diddle herself and all around the room you can hear losers whacking off in the dark. Last time I had to throw out my shoes afterward, because I'd stepped in so much man gravy (and no, not my own, but thanks for asking, a-hole). But Bono loves it. For years I've played along with him on this, but this time I tell him, "Buddy, please, let's take a rain check."

So here's the thing. We're driving down Route 280 in the rainstorm and this guy in a big Lexus sedan swerves as he's changing lanes, and almost hits us. Bono has this total Irish temper, plus he's shitfaced, and so he starts screaming and says, "Fook this, boyo, I'm gonna stick this fooking Aston Martin up this fooker's arse!" He floors it. In a nanosecond we're right on this guy's rear bumper with our high beams on. Then, I can't believe it, but *Bono hits the guy.*

Just a tap, the first time, but we're going about eighty and the Lexus starts fishtailing on the wet highway. The guy in the Lexus is freaking out, waving his arms. Bono cackles and he says, "How's dat fer a little taste of death, eh?" Then he pegs it and hits the guy again, harder this time, and then again, really hard, and the back of the Lexus crumples up like a tin can.

We all pull over. The guy gets out, and he's got blood coming out of his eye sockets he's so pissed. Then we open our doors and he sees who we are. It takes him a few seconds to register it. Then he's like, "Wait a minute, aren't you—and aren't you—"

We're standing there, like, "Uh huh, yup, that's right, and don't you feel like the world's biggest turd right now?" He says, "Dude, you guys scared the *shit* out of me! Oh, man! Ha! You guys are awesome! I'm soooo sorry about getting in your way, I mean seriously, if I'd known, you know, who you were or whatever."

Bono says, "Well, tink about dat next toim yer cuttin' off some bloke and you don't know who it is, right? Could be Jaysus. Or Boutros Boutros-Ghali or sumfin."

The guy gives him this look, like "Boutros who? Bootsie Collins? Huh?" And he says, "Seriously, I just want to say, I'm totally sorry about this."

Here's how classy Bono is. He goes over and shakes the guy's hand, the rocker handshake with the thumbs up, and he says, "Hey man, it's kewl, ya know? Seriously, apology accepted." Then Bono says, "Here, take this," and hands this guy his own personal iPod, the U2 model, in black. "You keep it," he says.

The guy looks at it for a second and he's like, "No friggin way." Like he just got a Cadillac from Elvis or something.

This is why I love Bono. Because down deep this is who Bono really is. This is the private Bono, the person the public doesn't get to see. He takes a moment that could turn ugly and he makes it into something really beautiful. That's just how his processor is wired, you know?

Bono, you are a class act. Totally.

So I'm getting huge blowback from the engineering department for firing Mike Dinsmore and his wise-ass helper Jeff. Apparently the engineers are all very devoted to the big carrot-top freak and they want him back. They've even signed a petition. But you know what? Frig that. I like firing people. I find it invigorating.

Whenever I'm feeling down, or low, or when I can't break through some negative energy and get back into a creative groove, one of the first things I'll do is fire someone. Naturally I try to be creative about it. One example is a game Lars Aki and I have created called Sniper. We do it when we need something to spark some creativity. Sniper is like a video game, only in meat space. Gist is, I'm John Allen Muhammad and Lars is my side-kick, Lee Malvo, and we go around looking for a victim. We make up some random rule. For example, the first person we meet with red hair gets fired. Or the first person wearing one of those stupid Bluetooth earpieces.

Today we're stuck trying to create some design ideas for the next-generation iMac computers, and so we head out onto the campus, with the rule for the day being that the first person who dares to speak to me without being spoken to—bam. In the neck. We start out in the headquarters building, then cross through the cafeteria and the iGym, past the climbing wall and the aquarium and the Zen center, then outside to the skateboard halfpipe and the mountain bike trails and the rifle range, back into the well-ness center, past the smoothie bar, the transgendered support group meeting, the aromatherapy room and the massage center where a squadron of therapists are rolling out their massage chairs for the afternoon shift.

Nobody will talk to us. Finally we give up and head back to the headquarters, where Paul Doezen comes rushing up.

"I've been looking all over for you. Your assistant said he didn't know where you were, and you didn't have your cell phone."

"Bam," Lars Aki says, shooting an invisible rifle at Paul. "You dead, sucka. You gone."

"Lars," I say, "we can't fire the CFO."

"The rules are the rules, dude."

"He's the CFO."

"What are you guys talking about?" Paul says.

"Nothing."

Lars gives me this disgusted look. "Dude, I'm going wind-surfing."

"What is it," I say to Paul as we ride up in the elevator.

"The shorts," he says.

"Whose shorts?"

"The short sellers. I gave you the spreadsheet. Remember?"

"Vaguely. Not really. What about them?"

"Short interest has doubled again. I've got a lead on who's doing it."

He gives me this look like a dog that's just fetched a stick and is waiting for praise. He's practically wagging his tail. But as I've explained before: I never give praise. Ever.

We get to the top floor and head to my office. I sit down. He starts to do the same, but I tell him to remain standing.

"I don't have time for a chat," I say. "Just tell me what you know."

"Company's registered in the Cayman Islands. Here."

He slides me a piece of paper. The name of the company is Ianus.

"Please tell me that's not some kind of joke about an anus," I say.

"Yah-nus," he says. "The Roman god. Also called Janus. It's where the word 'January' comes from."

"I knew that. But thanks for the history lesson. Who's behind it?"

"Hard to say. There's cut-outs inside of cut-outs, companies in the Caymans connected to companies in the Isle of Man. Shell companies, post office boxes, phone numbers that don't work anymore."

"Meaning?"

He shrugs. "Meaning we have no idea. Whoever's behind this knows what they're doing."

"Maybe it doesn't even matter. Who cares, right? Does it matter?"

"Your stock is your lifeblood. It's your oxygen. Someone's coming after it. I spent ten years on Wall Street. I know how these assholes operate. Someone is making war against you. We had some guys from Credit Suisse in the other day. They heard something about Microsoft trying to drive down the stock and buy the company on the cheap."

"That's crazy."

"Hey, Microsoft needs an operating system. But it could be anybody. Hedge funds, private equity guys. Maybe they figure they can bang us down, buy us cheap and then flip us. Who knows? I'm going to send a couple guys down to the Caymans, see what they can turn up. I can get Moshe to help. He's got some guys with intelligence backgrounds."

"Not Moshe. Leave him out of it. And keep this quiet. Don't use the company planes. Fly commercial. Pay cash for the tickets. Keep it off the expense sheets."

He gives me a look. "You worried there's someone inside?"

"Aren't you?"

He doesn't need to answer. Of course he is.

Short-sellers, leakers, competitors, U.S. Attorneys, SEC lawyers, in-house lawyers, conference organizers, beard colorists, couture consultants—all these distractions contribute to the random craziness that is always whirling around me and making it even more difficult for me to focus and concentrate on creating beautiful products. And now ever since we announced the SEC stuff we've been besieged by investment bankers and management consultants and every other kind of corporate advisory firm wanting to sell us some bullshit compliance services. It's like we've been hit by a car crossing the street and every blood-sucking ambulance-chasing lawyer in the world sees us as a sales opportunity.

I know people imagine that I just wander in here and think big thoughts and boom, invent the next iPod. I wish. There's way too much happening, way too many demands on my time.

Consider that after Paul leaves I find I've got four hundred and thirty two emails waiting for me, plus fifty-something WHILE YOU WERE OUT notes. These are unique WHILE YOU WERE OUT notes that I had created specially for me on handcrafted virgin pulp paper made from baobab trees in Madagascar. I spent a month looking at various kinds of paper pulp and then another month trying to pick the right shade of off-white and finally chose one called "Cotton Cloud" that is really pleasing to the eye.

The notes are arranged in order of importance. On top is a message from Steven Spielberg. Before I can even sit down and call him, my phone buzzes and it's Ja'Red saying he's got Spielberg's assistant on the line. I tell him fine, let me know when Spielberg is on the line and then patch me in. He comes back and says Spielberg's assistant wants me to get on the line first and then he'll go get Spielberg. I tell him to hang up. They call back and say, again, that Spielberg wants me to get on the phone first and then they'll patch him in. Again, I tell Ja'Red to hang up.

Finally, a few minutes later, Spielberg himself calls. He's acting all cool, like nothing happened. Whatever. Fine. Play it that way. He's also huffing and puffing and out of breath. He tells he's calling me from his treadmill, and do I mind if he puts me on speaker so he can work out while we talk. I tell him no, I don't mind, but let me put you on speaker too, and then I make a point of typing really loudly on my keyboard so he thinks I'm doing email instead of devoting my full attention to him. Honestly I hate all this dick-slapping that goes on in these calls but with the

Hollywood guys it's always like this. If you don't play along they figure they can walk all over you.

So Spielberg says that there is this huge war raging in Israel and Lebanon right now, but of course the American media isn't covering it at all. They'd rather report on Britney Spears putting her baby in the microwave. But it's totally serious, and totally bad. Spielberg has an idea for a DreamWorks-Pixar joint venture, an animated movie about two boys, one Israeli and the other Palestinian. Sort of *Schindler's List* meets *Aladdin* but using that funky humanoid animation from *Polar Express*. Elton John will write the songs.

"Okay," I say, "but will there be any talking fish? Talking cars? Some superheroes?"

Spielberg gets kind of sniffy and says, "I'm talking about serious *cinema verite* type animation."

I tell him he shouldn't start busting out the Latin words just because he knows I didn't go to college. He says, "It's French," and I'm like, "Whoa there, wait a minute, you're gonna make an animated movie *in French?* Are you kidding? Does Elton John even *speak* French? I mean, *Hello?* Is this really Steven Spielberg on the phone? Is this the guy who made *E.T.* and *Poltergeist?* Are you turning into Francis Ford Crapola or something? Because if that's the case, why not pull a Mel Gibson and do the whole movie in ancient Aramaic, or Maori, or that click-click language from Africa. Or Palestinian."

Thing about Spielberg is, he's a very cool guy and very brilliant and everything, but he tends to cop a huge 'tude with anyone who doesn't agree with his vision one hundred percent and do whatever he says.

"Steven," I say, "maybe I didn't go to film school, but trust me, I know what sells, right? I invented the friggin iPod, okay? Have you heard of it? So here's my idea. Instead of two boys we make it a boy and a girl, and we bump the age up a bit, like make them teenagers, so we can get a love story going, and we draw the girl really inappropriately hot, like in *Pocahontas,* and we put her in tight outfits or whatever, so we widen our audience and get some eighteen- to thirty-five-year-old males in the theater, not just kids. We cross-promote by having the characters wear iPods and we get a tie-in with McDonald's to make falafels with a movie theme wrapper."

Spielberg says nothing. He's cranking away on this treadmill. Finally he makes this big theatrical sigh and says, "Maybe we can talk later or something."

"Whatever," I tell him. "You're the one who called me, remember? So, like, good luck with your cartoon movie in Latin or whatever."

18

As if that's not bad enough, a few minutes later I get a call from Sir Richard Branson. The guy is crazy as a loon, I swear to God, and I never would have picked up my phone except I saw it was a call from England and I thought it might be Paul McCartney wanting to talk about getting the Beatles music onto iTunes. Instead I hear old Branson barking and I'm thinking, *Jesus Christ, first Spielberg, now this. Is there a full moon or something?*

"I'm up in my balloon!" he shouts, and I'm thinking, *Of course you are, you friggin twat, where else would you be?* For the life of me I will never understand what it is about rich guys and balloons.

"I'm on my satellite phone!" he screams. "I'm wearing a space suit and a helmet. We're at fifteen thousand feet, flying over northern Mongolia. Gorgeous. Can you hear me? Look, I've had this massive brainstorm. Can you hear me?"

I tell him I can't. He plows ahead anyway.

"Mate," he says, "here's my pitch and I'll get right to it. We're going to create a new section on Virgin Atlantic, right behind Upper Class, and call it iPod Class. The whole section is redone in that glossy white color like an iPod. The walls, the seat backs, the seat cushions, the carpet, the bathrooms, everything in bloody shiny white, like you're sitting smack inside an iPod. We throw in some fake champagne and cheap sushi and bang up the fare price by thirty percent over Coach, or Lower Class as we're now calling it. You're separated from everyone else by tinted plexiglass walls, so the punters in back can see you, and you just sit there looking cool and going, 'Yeah, how jealous are you lot, you'd love to be in here in iPod Class, wouldn't you, *as if.* Ha!'

"The message is, Look at me, I'm young, I'm cool, I'm obnoxious and *nouveau riche* and *arriviste,* I'm tech savvy, I'm a dotcommer, I own lots of cell phones and PDAs and gadgets, I live in Silicon Valley and I wear loafers without socks, I'm better than you, and when I fly . . . wait for it . . . I fly *iPod Class.* The chavs and the Irish'll go nuts for it. We'll get David Beckham and his wife to do the adverts."

"Richard, I don't get it. What's the iPod connection?"

"Hrm, well, uh, yah, whatever, who knows, but it's marketing innit? It's marketing. Like there's an Upper Class and now there's an iPod Class. It's all white, like an iPod. Geddit?"

The truth is I hate Branson because he made such a big deal about his stupid Virgin online music store and he was all Mr. Smack Talk about how he was gonna kick the crap out of iTunes, and now he's pretending he's my big "mate." Maybe the altitude is messing up his head and he figures I don't remember what a cockbreath he was on the music store.

So I push back and say I don't see the synergy and I don't want to dilute the brand, which I know is going to piss him off, because, as you might have noticed, old Branson has a teensy little ego problem.

Sure enough he gets all snippy and says in this fake plummy accent, "I'm sorry, did you say *dilute the brand?* My God I think I'm going to choke on a piece of *foie gras. Dilute the brand?* That'd be quite a feat, mate, diluting your brand. I mean I've been to your stores, Steve. The bloody Tivoli iPal? It's an FM radio! Only it's painted white and has a plug for an MP3 player. I don't hear you bitching about that, Steve."

By then he's practically screaming. I don't know if it's all an act or if he really is a complete psycho. I tell him, "Branson, my bro, cool out, do some yoga, smoke a doob, cut a fart in your space suit or whatever, but sure, go for it, set the controls for the center of the sun. Have the lawyers work it out and give old Steve a slice of the action. God bless you, you crazy goat-bearded bleached-hair balloon-flying freak."

"Bloody *right!*" he says. "Mate, you won't regret this! You can break the bottle of champagne on the first plane and take the maiden voyage, right alongside the Beckhams, my word as a gentleman."

I tell him thanks anyway, but I don't fly commercial, because it gives me hives and I'm allergic to non-vegans, but good luck. Then I call Paul Doezen and tell him, I don't care what you have to do, I don't care if you have to rent a MIG and fly up over northern Mongolia and shoot down his friggin balloon, but do *not* let this deal happen.

"Roger that," Paul says. "Oh, and by the way? We're rolling up the sales numbers for the quarter."

"And?"

"You're gonna be happy."

"Peace out," I tell him.

By now it's past seven and I'm looking out the window at the sun going down into the Santa Cruz Mountains, and I'd really like to drive out to Half Moon Bay and do some positive visualization exercises on the beach. Instead Ross Ziehm drags me down the hall to a conference call with some ding-dongs from Greenpeace who've got a hair across their butts because we use poisonous chemicals in our products.

"Folks," I say, "I don't think you understand. We're not making organic cereal here. We're not a vegetable company. We make computers and computer monitors. They have disk drives in them. And chips. Not much I can do about that. To make computers you need chemicals. And plastic. And glass. I can't make an iPod out of hemp. I can't rewrite the laws of gravity here."

The main guy, whose name is Pierre, starts hinting or suggesting or somehow talking in that roundabout European way about Apple making a bigger commitment to the cause of the environment. I know what this means. It's a shakedown. We give them more money so they can buy more boats to hassle tuna fishermen, and they'll stop bashing us in the press.

"How much?" I say.

"I'm sorry?"

"How much is it going to cost me to get you to leave me alone?"

He starts hemming and hawing and saying he thinks maybe there's been some misunderstanding, that's not what this call was about, blah blah blah.

"Pierre," I say, "I'm tired. It's late here. I've had a rough day. I don't want to fuck around. Just give me a number."

He asks me to hold for a moment. Then he comes back on. "Ten million?" he says.

"Done."

"Really?"

"I'll have my people make the arrangements."

"Mr. Jobs," he says "I want to thank you so much for your commitment to this noble cause, and you know, we are going to be soon redoing the list of the world's most greenest companies and I hope we will be seeing Apple moving well upward this year . . . "

He's still talking when I leave the room.

Great news. Our numbers roll in for the June quarter and they're huge. We do a conference call with the Wall Street asshats and blow away everyone's expectations. Better yet, according to Paul Doezen there's a reason I can't remember anything about the options. The reason is that I gave them all back, unexercised.

"The only thing I can find," Paul says, "is that maybe somebody put the wrong date on some of these things. But I can't see how that matters if you gave them back."

We're in the conference room, alone. He hands me a green folder which contains his report. The report consists of several pieces of paper which appear to contain columns of numbers and some words. More spreadsheets.

"Could you not have turned these into charts?" I ask. "Something visual? Something a normal person can understand?"

Paul just shrugs. He's a numbers guy.

I pretend to glance at the reports. Paul says he's not entirely certain that he's found everything, because he wasn't actually working at Apple when the backdating occurred—Zack Johnson was our CFO back then—but he's gone through the records and tried to put the puzzle together.

He's done this under my orders, entirely in secret. I don't want Charlie Sampson knowing that I'm conducting my own investigation on the side. Plus I figure if Paul does come up with something bad I can fire him and destroy whatever records he's found.

"So you're telling me this whole thing is over a clerical error?"

"Sort of," he says.

"So I'm off the hook."

"That's not actually what I said," Paul says.

"Well that's actually what I heard."

Paul says there still could be some issues about disclosure, and mwah mwah mwah. I don't know what it is about Paul, but sometimes when he gets going I just see that huge maw opening and closing and I'm aware that there is a sound coming out of him but it doesn't seem like words at all.

"What about the short sellers," I say.

He shrugs. "Still nothing. But if it's any consolation, who-ever's short has got their balls in a vise today. Have you seen the stock? It's going nuts."

He's right. The markets have closed but in after-hours trading our shares are surging. I turn on the TV and scan through the business channels. They're all raving about us. Of course they all mention the options stuff, but it's buried under the larger news, which is that our results blew everyone away.

Cramer, that lunatic, is pounding his desk and screaming at people to buy Apple.

"This stock is a must-own!" he says, his face so red it looks like his head is going to explode and splatter his brains all over the set.

"Steve Jobs should be elected president of the world!"

I'm so psyched that I drive down to the back of the parking lot and do some donuts in my Mercedes. There's smoke everywhere. A bunch of Mexican groundskeepers stand there whooping and waving their arms. One of them screams, *"Chinga tu puta madre, cabrón!"* which I believe means, "Dude, you totally rock!"

And you know what? I do. I totally do.

The reverie doesn't last long, however, because that evening, after flirting shamelessly with Ja'Red's girlfriend at the smoothie store in downtown Palo Alto and reconfirming my suspicions that she does, in fact, want to have hot, nasty monkey sex with me, I go outside and walk around a corner onto University Avenue and there, standing outside the Garden Court Hotel, is Tom Bowditch. Standing with him is Jim Bell, our COO. Right behind them, talking on a cell phone, is Charlie Sampson.

I duck into an alcove. I'm no expert on Machiavellian plots, but I'm pretty sure that when your second-in-command is holding secret meetings with your largest shareholder, and the lawyer who's investigating your company has come along for the ride, well, that isn't good.

I know I should march over there and confront them. But I can't. I just stand there, feeling dizzy. I lean against the doorway, half doubled over. I'm in front of a store called "Bodhi Tree— The Art of Gentle Living," which sells Buddhist knick-knacks. A bunch of little Buddhas are staring up at me.

One of the saleswomen from the store comes out and says, "Sir, can I help you? Are you okay? Sir? Do you need help? Should I call the police?"

Which in California is the way people say, "Yo, asshole, get the fuck out of our doorway or we'll call the cops."

Then she sees who I am and she gets all apologetic and says, "Oh, Steve Jobs! Namaste! Do you want to come in and have a glass of water?"

"I'm fine," I say. "Just looking at the, um, at the window."

I force a smile. I feel like I'm going to throw up.

Somehow I make it back to my car and get home, where sure enough there's a message Tom Bowditch. We're having an emergency board meeting, tomorrow morning, eight o'clock. I call him on his cell phone to find out what's going on. It rings through to voice mail. I leave a message. He doesn't call back.

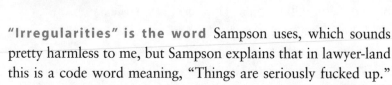

21

"Irregularities" is the word Sampson uses, which sounds pretty harmless to me, but Sampson explains that in lawyer-land this is a code word meaning, "Things are seriously fucked up."

We're in the boardroom and everyone is looking gray and washed out and scared shitless. It's the whole board of directors, with Al Gore once again joining via video link, plus Sampson and his team, and Paul Doezen, and Ross Ziehm. Even the old fartstain from the clothing store company is wide awake this time.

"What time period are we talking about?" the old guy says, which is what everyone else is wondering too, because if they were on the board when the "irregularities" took place, and if their signatures appear on the quarterly reports, then in the eyes of the law they're culpable.

In other words: it's save-your-own-ass time. The bad news is, from what Sampson has discovered so far, we're going to have to restate earnings back to 2001. Which means everyone on the board has some exposure. The dollar amounts aren't huge, but the SEC and the U.S. Attorney don't care if you're off by a penny or by a billion dollars.

"The fact is, there are problems," Sampson says. His helpers sit there looking proud of themselves, like they think maybe we should give them a bonus for doing such a fantastic bang-up job. I'd like to take them out and have them shot.

The clothing store guy puts his head in his hands. He starts to groan. I know what he's thinking, which is (a) why did I ever take this board seat, and (b) how much would it cost to have Steve Jobs killed, and (c) could we have it done in such a way that he'd die slowly and painfully?

The really bad news is that Sampson insists we have to announce this information to the public as soon as possible.

This is a huge problem. The timing could not be worse. Our biggest event of the year, the Worldwide Developers Conference, begins this weekend. We've spent months in rehearsals, working on presentations, getting products ready—and now all that work will be eclipsed by this stupid announcement.

"I really don't see why we can't push this back until after the conference," I say. "It's just going to distract everyone from what we're trying to convey at the show."

"There's no way you can wait," Sampson says. "You'd be withholding material information."

"I'm not saying wait forever," I say. "Just a week. Just let us have our conference, and then announce it."

"No dice," Tom Bowditch says. "Charlie's right. You can't hold stuff like this. That's exactly the kind of thing the SEC would go nuts over."

Tiny flecks of foam are piling up in the corner of Tom's mouth. He's giving me that crazy Rottweiler look, as if he's waiting for the others to leave so he can sink his teeth into my throat and tear me to pieces.

"So we're agreed?" Sampson says.

He's looking at Tom. He does not even pretend to address me.

"I'm not agreed," I say.

They ignore me.

"We're all set," Tom says.

The meeting breaks up. All of the board members hurry out of the room. None of them says good-bye to me. They won't even look at me.

Ross Ziehm pulls me aside and asks me if I want to go over the wording of the press release. I can't even speak. My heart is racing. I'm having this monster panic attack, this huge flashback to the eighties, and not the kind where you have a nightmare that you're walking into a meeting wearing Hammer pants. The nightmare I'm reliving is the one where the board threw me out of my own company. This was how it began. They started ignoring me in meetings, not even bothering to ask my opinion.

I hurry down the hall to my office. Ja'Red starts to tell me something about my yoga instructor, and how I missed my lesson and she wants to know if I want her to keep waiting or should she go home—but I wave him off.

"Hold my calls," I say.

I shut the door and lie down on my couch.

22

Before I can even recite my mantra the door blows open and tiny Tom Bowditch, our own little martinet, barges in, dragging Zack Johnson by the sleeve.

"Sit," Tom says to Zack, the way you'd tell a dog to sit. "There, on the couch, next to Rain Man. Good. Now look, you idiots. I want some fucking answers."

"I'd like some answers too," I say. "Like what were you and Jim Bell talking about at the Garden Court yesterday."

"Shut the fuck up." He turns to Zack and says, "Talk."

Zack was our CFO when this stuff happened. He's totally a stand-up guy and also, unfortunately, a guy who grew up with a pretty serious stuttering condition. He has spent years going to classes and worked really, really hard to get the impediment under control. But now, sitting here getting grilled by Tom, all those hours of speech therapy might as well have never happened.

"Well, um, ah, ah, ah, ah . . . wwww . . . wwww . . . ."

Tom says, "Spit it the fuck out, dummy, Jesus fucking Christ!" which is incredibly uncool and also serves only to make things worse.

Zack's face starts twitching. He's going, "Mmmmm . . . mmmmm . . . mmmmm."

So Tom says, "Okay. Look. Take a breath. Slow down. I'm sorry. I shouldn't have raised my voice."

Zack closes his eyes. Finally, in fits and starts, he explains how accounting can be this gray area and how some of these things may or may not have been okay back when we did them, but now the SEC is cracking down and getting tough and interpreting things in new ways.

"We gave out some options." He turns to me. "Remember? You got some of them. So did a bunch of other people. We backdated them to a point where the stock was cheap. This potentially enhanced the inherent value of the options. But also, the way we structured these grants enabled recipients to have a somewhat advantageous situation in regards to tax implications."

Tom says, "Can you say that in English?"

"Not really."

"So who did this?" Tom says. "Was it you? Did you do this? Why would you do something like this?"

"Steve told me to do it."

"No way," I say. "There's no way I ever told anyone to do anything like that."

"You did," Zack says. "You told me to do it. You gave me a direct order."

"I would never do that."

"You said you'd fire me if I didn't do it. And you'd spread some rumor in the Valley about me being fired for having kiddie porn on my office computer, so I'd never be able to work again. I distinctly told you it could be a problem."

"I don't remember this at all."

"I told you it wasn't really kosher and you said, 'Well, there's a difference between not really kosher and against the law, and is it against the law?' And I said, 'That would be a matter of interpretation.' And you said, 'Okay, then let's interpret it that it's legal.'"

"I would never say such a thing," I say. "No one at this company would do that. Not this company. You're not remembering correctly."

"I have notes on these conversations," Zack says.

Tom stands up. "All right. I've heard enough."

"So what do we do now?" I say.

"Good question, kid. I'll tell you what. You know that lotus position? My advice is you should go into your meditation room, get into that position, put your head between your legs and kiss your ass goodbye."

"Nice," I say. "Funny."

"And by the way, what the fuck are you thinking, firing your head of engineering on the iPhone?"

"What, now Dinsmore is calling you?"

"People called me on his behalf. And yes, I met with him. Are you crazy? This guy is your best engineer. He's running the project. And you take him off? Why?"

"Insubordination," I say. "He refused to fire someone."

"Did it occur to you that the someone he didn't want to fire was also crucial to the project?"

"Nobody is indispensable."

"You of all people should keep that in mind, kid. Because you know what? I know what you did. You double-dipped. Wasn't enough for you to get ten million shares. You had to back-date them, too, and try to squeeze out a little extra out of it. You guys out here all act like California is a different country or something. Maybe you figure nobody in Washington actually reads those little forms you send in every quarter. Maybe you figured nobody would care, or that they'd give you a pass because you're the Great Steve Jobs. Well, you're wrong. You're in deep shit, kid. Deep, deep shit."

I ask Tom what he'd do if he were in my shoes.

He says, without missing a beat, "I'd leave the country."

23

Later on, I'm getting ready to go home when Paul Doezen shows up carrying his MacBook. "There's something you need to see," he says.

He pulls up the Yahoo! Finance page and goes to our message board.

"See this guy?" he says, pointing to a commenter who calls himself *socratech*. "He's a basher. He's up here all the time. Look."

He clicks some button that pulls up a list of every post this guy has made about us. He's put up more than fifteen hundred items in the past two months.

"So he's a nut," I say. "The world's full of them."

"Maybe. But look here."

He opens up the guy's latest item, posted an hour ago:

> Reliable source sez Apple board held secret emergency meeting this afternoon. Bad news found!!! TBA later this week & will tank the stock hard fer sure. Word to the wise, take yr profits & clear yr positions on this overhyped POS before the proverbial shit hits the proverbial spinning blades.

"Someone's talking," Paul says. "Which, okay, that happens. Usually I'd say it's just random. Someone tells their wife, or goes to lunch and tells their friend. Not supposed to do that, but it happens, and word travels. But this," he says, pointing to the screen, "this is different. This guy puts up fifteen hundred items about us, all negative. Now he knows when our board meets?

And he knows what they say? This guy's working for someone. Somebody's feeding him."

My phone buzzes. It's Ja'Red. He says he has Ross Ziehm on the line, and it's urgent.

"Put him through," I say.

"Are you alone?" Ross says.

"I'm here with Paul. You're on speaker."

"Okay. Look, there's a story on the Dow Jones wire. I'm going to send you a link on iChat. Here. You got it?"

There's a *ping* as the message arrives. I pull up the page and glance at the headline: "Trouble found at Apple." It's a six-paragraph story based on "sources close to the matter" saying that Apple was about to announce that its internal investigation had turned up problems regarding backdated options.

"I'm already getting calls," Ross says.

I tell him to come up. We try to figure out who's leaking. Paul thinks it could just be that the Dow Jones reporter saw the Yahoo message and ran with it.

"Can't be," Ross says. "They wouldn't run without their own source."

"So whoever told the Yahoo guy also told the Dow Jones reporter."

"Probably. And whoever it is, it's someone that Dow Jones trusted, or else they wouldn't run the story. It's someone who knows what they're talking about, and is actively trying to put this out there."

Ross says it must be a board member, but he can't imagine anyone on the board being stupid enough to do something like that.

"It's not a board member," I say. "It's Sampson. Or one of his guys. It's got to be."

"Why them?" Ross says.

"You saw him in the board meeting. That fight about

whether we could hold the news until after the developers conference. He figures I want to stall. He's trying to force our hands."

"We told him we'd put it out now."

"Maybe he wants to make sure. Maybe he's trying to send us a message."

"I don't know."

"Lawyers are the worst leakers in the world. Look at any merger talks that get leaked, it's always the lawyers."

"There's at least two dozen people who know there was a meeting," Paul says. He's got a yellow legal pad and is making a list. "Figure everyone on the board, plus whoever keeps their schedules for them. Plus all the chauffeurs and pilots and travel agents. Sampson and his three guys, plus their admins and assistants. The people in my office. The people in your office. Anyone in PR who's been brought in to work on the release."

"We could pull the phone logs," Ross says. "And search the email system. Steve?"

I don't answer. I'm looking out the window, out over the rooftops of Cupertino, toward Homestead High, where I went to school, and, past that, the neighborhood in Los Altos where I grew up. I'm thinking about the day when we first moved the company out of my parents' house and into a real office building on Stevens Creek Boulevard. I was twenty-two years old. Our delivery system was a ten-year-old Plymouth station wagon. Our biggest concern was keeping the car running. I miss those days.

PART TWO

Dark Night of the Steve

24

My parents did not hide the fact of my adoption from me. I always knew. So did our neighbors. So did their kids. When I was seven years old the taunting began. In the schoolyard, in the street. Until then I had not given any thought to what it meant to be adopted. But now, stung by teasing, it hit me. My birth parents, a pair of snooty intellectual graduate students, had taken one look at me and said, "No thanks." They gave me up. They abandoned me.

You do not need to be a trained psychologist to understand what this does to a person. Shame? You have no idea. That word does not begin to describe it. I would hide under my bed. I would cry and refuse to come out. I would lie on my back, with my eyes closed, trying to will myself into becoming invisible. I prayed—in those days I believed in God—that I could fall asleep and wake up a different person.

I became obsessed with adoption narratives. Especially those in which an orphan grows up to accomplish great deeds. Jane Eyre. Cinderella. Oedipus. Romulus and Remus. Pip in *Great Expectations*. Siegfried in Norse mythology. Krishna. Little Orphan Annie—I followed her adventures every day in the *San Jose Mercury News*.

My favorite was Superman. Born on another planet, raised by humble parents, secretly possessing superhuman abilities. I devoured the comic books. I sat transfixed on the floor watching the old black-and-white TV show with George Reeves. I became convinced that I, too, was a kind of Superman. I suppose this was my way of coping with the shame, compensating for the loss.

I saw myself as a hero. As different. Better than the people around me. A savior, destined to do great things.

Was I also bitter? Yes. Am I still? Very much so. But I have learned to transform my bitterness into fuel. I have harnessed my anger, the way a hydroelectric plant harnesses the force of a river.

Every day I tell myself that somewhere out in the Midwest there are two snobby academics who gave birth to the greatest figure of our age, but they were so self-absorbed and short-sighted that they could not recognize their son's inherent coolness.

These two fools could have had a son who's worth five billion dollars. They could be zooming around in the world in a private jet, zipping from their ski house in Aspen to their island in Tahiti.

That's right, you jerks. You're the Pete Best of parents. I hope you enjoy living out your days in some cut-rate assisted-living facility, eating creamed chip beef on toast. Yum.

25

Twice a year I get to play messiah, arriving in an auditorium filled with people who worship me like a living god and hang on every word I say. These people spend huge amounts of money and travel from all around the world to see me in person. Some of them camp out overnight, sleeping on the sidewalk, so they can be first to get into the auditorium when the doors open in the morning.

The first event where I do this is Macworld, which is a conference we created for ordinary run-of-the-mill dweebs who use Macs. The second and more prestigious is our annual Worldwide Developers Conference, which is aimed at the guys—and yes, they are almost all guys—who write software that runs on our computers and have built companies around our machines. They're mostly middle-aged dweebs, fat and pasty. An alarmingly high percentage wear ponytails and travel with short-scale guitars so they can have jam sessions in their hotel rooms and record themselves using our GarageBand software and upload their songs onto .mac homepages. Sad. I know.

"Look at them out there," Ross Ziehm says. "Talk about pathetic."

"You think they'll give me shit about the options?"

"I'd be shocked if they didn't."

It's Friday evening, three days before the developers conference kicks off, and we're hosting a special dinner for one hundred of our biggest partners. We've rented out a Shinto temple in Campbell, near our headquarters. Ja'Red and I are hanging out backstage with Ross, waiting for the dorks to get seated.

Talk about bad timing. Last night we put out the release saying that we'd found some irregularities in our accounting. The story was in every newspaper this morning, and has been on TV shows all day. All the stories zoomed in on me. Steve Jobs, criminal mastermind. Will he step down? Can Apple survive without him? Our stock is getting clobbered. And somewhere, in some cramped kitchen, Francis X. Doyle must be creaming in his relaxed fit jeans.

"Just stick to the script," Ross says.

I pull back the curtain and peek out. I never get stage fright, but suddenly I'm getting butterflies.

"They look hostile," I say.

"They're fine. They love you. They worship you. You just have to reassure them, that's all."

Ja'Red hands me a bottle of water, and then pats my face with a towel and brushes me with some powder to take off any shine. I peek out again. Unlike most companies, which dish out Australian lobster tails and bottles of hundred-year-old cognac at events like this, at Apple we bring them to a temple and serve miso soup, brown rice and steamed vegetables. Tiny portions. To drink, just water. After dinner, hot water with lemon. No alcohol, no caffeine, no sugar.

Tonight I wish we were serving tequila shots and hits of four-way blotter acid. But no. The Apple faithful want answers. At times like these the cult leader has to step up and reassure the flock.

So we let the dweebs get seated. We make them wait. The suspense builds. Then we zap the house lights, smash a gong, and there, on stage, in a spotlight, like Buddha in blue jeans, I appear.

The room goes silent. I stand there. I look at them. I press my hands together. I'm wearing my patented JobsWear outfit: jeans, black turtleneck, and rimless eyeglasses that cost more than most of these guys make in a month. I keep looking at them. I make sure they can feel my power. They are small, I am large. They are followers, I am the leader.

"Welcome," I say. "Namaste. Peace."

I bow, and smile. There's a smattering of nervous applause. I wait again. I let them look at me. I let them see that I'm not afraid. I look left. I look right. I do this stiffly, self-consciously, as I always do. I pretend that I am making eye contact with individuals when really I am looking just over their heads.

Finally I speak.

"Options," I say. "That's what everyone wants to talk about. You've read the papers. You've seen the news on TV. What's the big story today? The reliability of OS X? The new iLife suite of software applications? The new iPhoto, which can hold fifty thousand photos? Fifty. Thousand. Photos. Is this what they're writing about? Nope. Not the things we're doing to exploit Intel's dual-core architecture and 64-bit computing, either. Not our roadmap for quad-core chips, and our next-generation bus architecture. Nope. Let's talk about options. Let's drop all sorts of innuendoes. Let's imply that maybe people have cheated, or lied, or committed crimes. Let's *gossip*."

They sit there looking ashamed of themselves. Perfect. So now I flip it around on them.

"You know what? I don't blame you. You love this company. You want to know that everything is all right. That is what I am here to tell you. Everything. Is. All. Right. We have not done anything wrong. Of this I can assure you."

I glance backstage at Ross Ziehm. He gives me a thumbs up.

A guy in back puts up his hand.

"They said in the *Journal*—"

I cut him off.

"That story was unauthorized. We did not give the *Journal* permission to print that story. It was full of inaccuracies. We told them not to print it and they went ahead anyway."

Another guy says, "In your press release you said there were irregularities. Can you expand on that?"

I look down at my hands. I smile like a patient Zen master. It's the look that's meant to convey that although this guy is brain-damaged I will be tolerant of him because I'm such an amazing human being.

"Sir," I say, "I'm no expert, but from what I'm told, that term is a way of indicating that there is nothing seriously wrong. As you probably know, I don't care about money. I care only about creativity. I care about making beautiful objects. That's my passion. You wanted beautiful iMacs. Boom, we delivered. You wanted a smaller iPod. Boom, we created the Nano and the Shuffle. You wanted video. Boom, we gave you built-in cameras and free videoconferencing software on all Macs. Now look. I'm not a lawyer. I'm also not an MBA. I have those people on my staff, and they take care of stock market stuff. What I am is an artist. Like Andy Warhol. You think people ever hassled Andy Warhol about stock options? Man oh man."

Hands keep flying up.

"Are you going to step down?"

"Absolutely not."

"If you do step down, who will run the company? What's your succession plan?"

"I'm not going to step down. The question is moot."

"But if you did."

I glance at Ross. He's already talking into the microphone on his wrist, instructing our Israelis to get this guy out of the room.

I give the dead man my biggest smile.

"I won't step down," I say. "Never, ever. I'm Dictator for Life."

That gets a few laughs.

"There are rumors about criminal charges."

"Not true."

"And the U.S. Attorney?"

"I've heard nothing about that."

"Why have some of your management team hired criminal defense attorneys?"

"You'll have to ask them," I say, which is a lousy answer, and as soon as I say it I can see Ross wince and I want to take it back, but it's too late.

"Is it true you fired Mike Dinsmore?"

Jesus, the Dinsmore thing again. I realize the guy's a legend, but I didn't realize he had a friggin fan club.

"Mike resigned," I say. "I don't feel comfortable discussing personnel issues here."

It's just starting to feel like it could get out of hand when Ja'Red, who's made his way out into the audience and is dressed like a developer—ratty T-shirt, oversized shorts—puts up his hand and asks, "Is it true you're going to announce a wide-screen iPod with a 100-gigabyte hard drive on Monday?"

"No comment," I say, which of course makes these bozos think it must be true, even though it isn't.

They burst into crazy applause, the kind that goes on and on and won't stop. Next thing I know they're rising up out of their chairs and cheering. I love Apple developers. Honestly, I really do.

26

Saturday morning things take a turn for the worse. Bob Iger calls me at home and says Disney has also discovered problems with backdated options. The problems are rooted in the Pixar division, which they bought from me.

"We just put out a release. It'll be in the papers tomorrow," he says.

Sure enough, there it is on Sunday morning, front page of all the Sunday papers and up on the TV news. The idiots on Fox can barely contain their glee. They're having a field day with this, saying Steve Jobs is going to jail and maybe he should call Martha Stewart, maybe she can teach him how to make a shiv out of a toothbrush, ha ha. I flip to CNN, CNBC, the three networks—they're all making hay on this. I switch to ESPN, and I swear to God, some guy on a sports show brings it up. Some basketball player has been arrested for drug possession, and the announcer says, "Maybe he can share a cell with Steve Jobs of Apple Computer. Have you heard about that? Seriously, it's some bad stuff. These computer nerds, you gotta watch them. They'll hack in and cook the books."

On Sunday Iger calls again and says the Disney board is going to meet later this week. I've never really liked Iger. Put it this way. He began his career as a weatherman, and it shows. He's fine as long as he's standing up reading from a script. Try to have a conversation with him, and there's just nothing there. Nice guy, sure. But no passion. No imagination. But now we're business partners because he was crazy enough to offer me seven and a half billion dollars for my company. I knew it would be a pain in the ass to have to work with these sphincters, but there was no way to reject the offer. The price was too high. The deal made me Disney's biggest shareholder and got me a seat on the board. But all that means is that now I have to schlep down to Los Angeles, a city that I hate, and listen to these movie guys yap. And yap. And yap.

"How bad is it gonna be?" I ask him.

"If you own a bulletproof vest," he says, "I'd say bring it."

I spend the rest of the day Sunday fielding phone calls from people who hate me. They're loving this, of course. Bill Gates says he's going to send me a book on how to survive in prison. Michael Eisner, who's still pissed because I helped push him out of Disney, pretends he hasn't seen the stories and is just calling to say hello. "I'm out in the Hamptons," he says. "I'm doing a crossword puzzle and I need some help. Buddhist word, five letters, starts with K. Kurma? Korma? No, that's some kind of Indian food. Oh wait. *Karma.* That's it, isn't it? Karma. Like if you do something bad to someone, like really fuck someone over, it comes back to bite you, right? Well, glad you're doing so well these days. Couldn't be happier for you. You get my drift? Peace out, as the kids say."

Worst of all, I get a call from Al Gore informing me of his intention to step down from the Apple board.

"It's not because I think being on your board is going to hurt my reputation," he says. "I really think Apple is a fantastic company. But you know, I've got so much on my plate these days, what with the global warming and all, and I'm still maybe gonna make a run in 2008, which is going to demand even more of my time. So I'm just way too busy. Really, really, really busy. So are we okay on this?"

I call Tom Bowditch on his mobile number. Turns out he's in town, staying at the Garden Court. He comes over to my house and we get Al Gore on a conference call. Tom tells Al that he can't quit, and that if he even mentions quitting again Tom will have him kidnapped and castrated.

"We're all in this together," Tom says. "You're not going to run out on us the way you abandoned Clinton when he got into trouble."

"I didn't abandon Bill Clinton," Al says.

"Please. You dropped him like he was on fire."

Tom was against putting Al Gore on the board from the start. He said Al was (a) an idiot, and (b) too divisive. I figured it would be cool to have the former vice president on our board. Plus he's got this big global warming crusade going, so he makes us seem more progressive.

"Bill Clinton let the American people down," Gore says. "He disappointed all of us."

"The guy got a blowjob. Big fucking deal. And you ran screaming for cover like a prissy little girl."

"That blowjob cost me an election. The guy ruined my career."

"Think what you need to think to get to sleep at night," Tom says. "But we're not letting you jump ship. You're going to stay and do your job. You're going to defend this company. Christ, you're the reason we're in this mess."

"Excuse me?"

"You know where this is coming from. This isn't about some asshole U.S. Attorney in San Francisco. I've been talking to people. This is coming from Washington. The Bushies hate you. They figure they can tar you with this scandal and ruin you for 2008. Meanwhile the rest of us get caught in the crossfire."

"That's the most ridiculous thing I've ever heard."

"What's ridiculous is you dragging us into this mess and then trying to scoot when the shit hits the fan. You're on the board of this company. You're not leaving. You get it?"

Al sputters and pouts for a while and says he's never been talked to like this in his entire life, not even by Hillary.

"You're staying on the board," Tom says.

"Whatever."

"Say it. I want to hear you say it."

Al does his big sigh and says, "I'm staying on the board."

"Good. And fuck you for trying to leave."

Tom hangs up. He spends the rest of the day at my house, foaming at the mouth and spraying me with spit, chewing me out for being such a dumb-ass.

After all this, on Monday morning I have to give my keynote address. I'm standing on stage at the Moscone Center and we've got the whole Leni Riefenstahl *Triumph of the Will* thing going, with the giant "X" on the wall behind me and huge seventy-foot images flashing on screens, and five thousand glassy-eyed geeks are hanging on my every word and ready to go out into the streets and kill for me if I ask them to. Usually

I'd feel like the king of the world, but today I'm losing it. Just losing it.

This may be in part because our rehearsals have been so rocky. We had problems with my beard, first of all. Annalisa, my colorist, has been trying out some new products and the mix of salt versus pepper is off by three percent, and in the wrong direction—I'm too gray. The other problem involved my mock turtlenecks. My regular supplier had its factory wiped out in some tsunami. Katarina, my couture consultant, went looking for a replacement but couldn't find the right texture. In the rag trade they call this the "hand" of the fabric. I rehearsed wearing a bunch of different shirts and couldn't find anything that felt right. It's not that anyone in the audience can tell the difference. But I'll know, and it throws me off.

The other problem we had was with the rehearsal space itself. We gutted one of our buildings on the Cupertino campus and built an exact replica of the conference hall at the Moscone Center and hired five thousand people to sit in the audience for a month and pretend to be Apple developers. (We give them Nembutal to give them that glazed, worshipful look, and we flash lights at them when it's time to cheer wildly.) But there was something wrong. I kept telling Simon, our event producer, "This space is not correct. There are too many seats." He insisted they'd built the space using the Moscone Center blueprints. Sure enough, however, when we sent one of our VPs up to San Francisco to check, it turned out that after they built the Moscone Center they removed two seats in the second-to-last aisle. So we pulled out two seats to match, but by then it was the last day of rehearsal.

So, yeah. I'm up here not feeling too good.

I'm supposed to stay on stage for two hours, running through demos and receiving standing ovations for minor enhancements to existing products. Instead I keep running off the stage, struck by panic attacks. Ja'Red fans me with a towel and tells me I'm doing great, while Lars Aki and Jim Bell go out and cover for me. We all try to pretend that things are going according to plan, but people can tell something is wrong.

By Monday afternoon the bloggers who follow us are freaking out saying they think I have cancer again, because I looked so gaunt and worn out. You know what? You'd look worn out too if you'd had the kind of weekend I did.

Worse yet, I don't even have time to think about it, because as soon as I walk off the stage I get into a car and drive to San Jose and hop into the Jobs Jet for a trip to China. I'm a terrible traveler. Always have been. Just going to the East Coast messes me up, no matter how much melatonin I take. Anything beyond that, like Asia or Europe, and I'm a zombie.

I'm going to China to try to undo some bad publicity that we've been getting because the manufacturing company that builds our iPods supposedly has some labor problems in a plant in Longhua. Some British tabloid reported that the workers there are making only fifty bucks a month and working fifteen-hour days and getting no breaks for tea and crumpets and no free backrubs either, boo friggin hoo. Frankly I don't think this is my problem. We don't own this plant. We just buy from them. It's out in the middle of nowhere in this new industrial region, a landscape of mud and shit where the rivers have all been poisoned with chemicals and the air stinks and the sky has been charred black by smokestacks and cars and trucks chuffing exhaust from diesel fuel and leaded gasoline. *It's like a vision of hell*—that's what I'm thinking as we're flying in to their crappy little airport, though Ja'Red, who's sitting across the plane looking out the other side, seems to think it's totally amazing.

"I can't believe I'm in China," he says. "I mean, China! Right? I can't believe it! Wow. *China.* I can't believe it."

I suppose he thinks it's going to be like going to Chinatown in San Francisco, with fortune cookies after every meal. He's in for a big disappointment, which is partly why I brought him.

"Dude," I say, "get a grip."

The one cool thing about being a super-rich Westerner arriving anywhere in the developing world is that you always get this huge reception, with lots of wreaths and flowers, and endless speeches by the local big shots. It's all good, as long as you're super vigilant and don't actually touch anyone.

Roughly half of the population of the province appears to be waiting for us when we get off the plane. After the speechmaking all I have to do is ride to the plant and show my face to some pack of reporters and say that we're conducting an audit and working to ensure that the plant adheres to our high standards, mwah mwah mwah. It's all a publicity stunt, and as soon as I'm done making my statement I want to zip back to the Jobs Jet and get the hell out of there. But the plant manager insists I go on a tour of the dorms where the workers live, so I can see how great the conditions are. I tell him there's no need for that, and then there's a bunch of back-and-forth and angry jibber-jabber in Chinese, and finally Ross Ziehm informs me that the manager will be deeply insulted if I just leave and that if we don't visit the dorm we're going to offend the honor of the country and create some huge international incident. So in we go. "Just smile and keep moving," Ross tells me.

The walls are freshly painted and the dorm reeks of bleach, as if it's just been scrubbed for our visit. The workers are young. They're in their teens and early twenties. They're scrawny. Clearly they've been told to smile and look happy, and they're making a great effort in this regard. They're lined up in rows and turned out for inspection, which unfortunately makes them look a little bit like prisoners, which I don't think is the impression that our hosts are trying to convey. Each room houses one hundred workers. They sleep on small metal beds that butt up against each other, head to foot, four beds deep. Each bed has a thin mattress on a metal spring. The blankets are thin, ratty, patched with scraps of cloth. Quilts, I guess you'd call them, if you were absolutely full of shit. The workers are standing at attention, and they're all wearing T-shirts, mostly from America—used clothing that's been shipped over in containers, sold by the ton.

"Dude, awesome!" Ja'Red says to a kid who's wearing a Phish T-shirt, and I'm not sure but I think Ja'Red believes the kid is a big fan of Phish, like maybe Ja'Red figures these kids all own eighty-gigabyte iPods and sit around at night downloading music and movies from the iTunes music store over their free high-speed broadband WiFi routers. I don't have the heart to tell him. He and the kid are now trading high fives.

The translator proudly informs us that even after paying rent to live in the dorm a good worker can easily make more than two dollars for a fifteen-hour workday. The translator also says that all of the workers are at least sixteen years old. In fact they look very much like the teenagers who hang out on University Avenue in Palo Alto with skateboards and cell phones, only slightly less miserable and surly. One of them, this skinny dude with a messed-up harelip and big huge eyes like a kid in some Margaret Keane painting, keeps staring at me with this weird tranquil expression on his face. He's wearing a faded T-shirt with a picture of Elmo from *Sesame Street*. He's standing with his hands at his sides. I look into his big dark eyes and read his thoughts and discover, to my dismay, that he believes we're from some do-gooder organization like Amnesty International and that we're here to bring him home to his village. He's looking at me with those huge eyes and thinking: "Thank you."

The translator breezes along, pointing out how clean the dorms are and how each worker has his own bucket for washing his clothes and his own two-foot-by-two-foot locker for storage.

He tells us how happy and proud these workers are to be sending money home to their families and how grateful they are to Apple for giving them this opportunity.

When we get to the door I look back at that kid with the messed-up lip. He's gazing at me with those big eyes, looking betrayed.

"Just smile and keep moving," Ross Ziehm says, pulling my arm. "Smile and keep moving."

Ja'Red, following behind, is slapping high fives with all the kids, moving down the line like he's some kind of rock star greeting his fans.

Back outside, I put on a fake smile and talk to the reporters again, and the whole time I'm feeling my soul curling up inside me, huge pieces of it shriveling and dying.

From Longhua we fly to Beijing for a meeting with some government ministers, and we all work very hard, on both sides, to make sure we say nothing of any real significance. Then we're off to Taiwan for a meeting with the top guys at the parent company that owns the manufacturing plant in Longhua. They're scared that we're going to pull our contract, so they offer us a twenty percent price cut; we were only going to ask for ten.

Next is Tokyo for a meeting with Sony, because we use their batteries in our laptops and the things have been overheating and blowing up. Sony hates us because they know we're moving in on their turf in consumer electronics, but we're a big customer of their component division and they can't afford to lose our business. So they're stuck. To show their contrition the Sony bozos make us endure a tour of the facility where Sony builds laptop batteries, so they can show off all the new processes and safeguards they've put in place. Honestly, I haven't a clue what any of this stuff is about, and by this point I'm so messed up with jet lag and sleep deprivation that for a moment I'm thinking we're back in China at the factory run by teenagers.

I'm dead. I'm exhausted. Back on the jet, I get into bed. But now, of course, I can't sleep. I keep thinking of that kid with the messed-up lip. He's haunting me. I close my eyes and see his face. Ja'Red brings me an Ambien. When I wake up we're in Moscow, where I attend the grand opening of an Apple retail store. Everyone is effusive and happy. Men with beards are bear-hugging me and kissing me on both cheeks. I'm foggy from the Ambien and I can't understand a word anyone says. The moment we're back in the car I've forgotten who we met and why we were there.

Next stop is Paris for a meeting with Vivendi. We discuss music downloads, I think. Next we fly to London to meet Yoko Ono and beg her, for the millionth time, to stop being an idiot and let us sell Beatles music on iTunes. But when we get there we find out Yoko has flown back to New York. At the airport we cross paths with Howard Stringer of Sony, who was just hosting us in Tokyo. I believe we have a meal together in London. I have a hazy memory of being in a restaurant with him.

From London we chase Yoko to New York, only to be told, after we've driven all the way into the city, that she needs to reschedule. She does this on purpose to drive people nuts. It's a negotiating tactic. Back to Teterboro we go, and I take another Ambien and sleep until we land in Los Angeles, where somehow, by some magic, it is only Thursday evening. I don't know how that's possible.

I've never been able to take Disney board meetings seriously. First of all we sit around a conference table whose legs are carved to look like the Seven Dwarves from Snow White. These are intended to match the pillars holding up the roof on the outside of the headquarters building, which are also Disney cartoon figures, only they're nineteen feet tall. Who can work in a place like this? Everywhere you go there are pictures of Mickey and Minnie and Goofy. Face it. It's weird.

I used to think the movie business would be kind of glamorous. In fact most of the work gets done in crappy-looking office parks or on lots that have all the charm of an airplane hangar. At the executive level these companies are run by moronic MBAs, just like every other big company. Talk to any BlackBerry-toting movie-company vice president and you might as well be visiting a company that makes cars, or potato chips, or pharmaceuticals. If you're wondering if this is why so many movies suck so badly, it is.

At the board level it's even worse. Most movie companies are run by absolute idiots. Disney's board includes a guy from an electric utility; a guy from a cosmetics company; a guy from Sears; a guy from a liquor company; a guy from Procter & Gamble; a guy from Starbucks; a Latina lady from some Mexican newspaper who's here, let's face it, because she knocks down two diversity categories with one shot; a guy from a software company that's practically out of business; and a woman whose big claim to corporate fame is that she used to work at Cisco Systems.

Now these mental giants, these paragons of virtue, these captains of industry, are sitting around the Mickey Mouse table drumming their fingers and giving me dirty looks. And I'm feeling sick. Not metaphorically, but literally. Ja'Red and I spent the night at Larry's house in Malibu. I broke into the liquor cabinet and drank too much vodka, trying once again to erase the image of that kid in Longhua. I slept on the couch, in my clothes, and woke up with creatures chasing each other around inside my intestines. Larry's housekeeper was cooking eggs. I ran to the bathroom and threw up.

"Steve," Iger says, "nobody's saying this is your fault. We're just saying that as the guy who was running Pixar, and the guy who I presume is most intimately familiar with how that company was run, you're going to have to be our point man on this issue. And so we'd like it if you could kind of walk us through what happened with regard to these options and various other issues regarding compensation. But as I said, nobody is saying it's your fault."

Translation: It's your fault.

Whatever. Now I'm actually grateful that I'm hung over. I try to explain to them what happened. I tell them how a few years ago John Lasseter started making noise about leaving Pixar. He was making these threats, ironically enough, because Disney was trying to lure him away.

Thing is, John Lasseter was the creator of *Toy Story*. He's the greatest animator who ever lived, a genius on the level of Leonardo da Vinci or Michelangelo.

There was no way we were going to lose him. So we wrote John a new contract, with a huge bonus, a huge raise, and a load of stock options. To sweeten things a little bit more we backdated the options so they'd be more valuable. He stayed. He went on to make *Finding Nemo* and *The Incredibles*, both of which won Oscars and raked in hundreds of millions of dollars for us.

"My opinion? I think we did the right thing," I say. "You can hate me if you want to, but I will not apologize for keeping John Lasseter attached to Pixar. Also, has it not occurred to you that the reason I had to do what I did was that you guys, right here at Disney, were trying to poach him away from Pixar? Do you realize that? If anything, this mess is *your* fault. You guys caused it. Now you're trying to blame me. I think you should all be ashamed of yourselves."

Rule Number One when talking to people who think they're powerful is this: Insult them. Tell them they're stupid. Challenge them. Unlike the rest of the world, they're not used to this kind of abuse. Nobody ever talks to them like this. The disrespect knocks them back on their asses real fast.

Sure enough Iger starts backpedaling about how there's no need to get angry here or to make personal attacks but we need to figure out how to solve the problem, blah blah, so I cut him off and say, "Robert, you know not whereof you speak. Please stop talking. Are you done? Good. Now I'd like you to take a deep breath, and hold it, and don't let it out until I say so."

Then, in a matter of seconds, I hypnotize the other frigtards, and in an extremely patronizing voice, a voice you might use when talking to a group of third graders, I explain that I want them all to go home tonight and sit down in a quiet place and do some real soul-searching. "Look into your hearts," I say, "and ask yourselves how you really feel about what you've all tried to do to me here today. If you want to apologize to me now, you can. Or you can send me a note later. Or a phone call. Thank you for your time. I won't be taking questions. Goodbye."

That's it. I walk out. In the car on the way to the airport I gaze out the window at the palm trees and the garish buildings and I wonder how anyone lives here. I hate Los Angeles. I always have. I hate all of the people here. The fawning, the flattery, the obvious insincerity, the constant backstabbing. What really bugs me is the way people kiss my ass everywhere I go. Sure, the adulation is nice. But they worship me for the wrong reasons. They don't have any idea of who I am or what I've accomplished. All they know is that they've seen me on TV or in the pages of *Vanity Fair.* I'm famous. If they're slightly more clued in they know that I ran Pixar and I'm the biggest shareholder in Disney; so, in their miserable little movie business, which as far as anyone down here is concerned is the only business that exists, I'm a big shot.

Never mind that Apple alone is twice the size of the entire U.S. box office for all movies combined. Never mind that the computer industry as a whole dwarfs all of Hollywood, and that no movie studio will ever make the kind of profit margins that a software company like Microsoft does. Never mind that the morons who run the movie business have created a high-cost, high-risk business model that any clever child could tell you makes no sense, and that ninety-five percent of what they do involves churning out garbage and praying it sells. No, down there they really believe their own hype. They really believe they're important, and that what they do matters.

On the jet I sleep. By Friday evening I'm home in Palo Alto and seriously considering selling my shares in Disney and walking away from the movie business altogether.

"Who needs the hassle?" I tell Mrs. Jobs, as we're doing our bedtime yoga. "For that matter, maybe I should quit Apple too. See how well they do without me."

"They wouldn't last a year," she says.

I tell her about the kid in Longhua, the one who kept staring at me.

"Poor you," she says. "You shouldn't have to see that."

"I know, right?"

I've been giving some thought to the China situation and how we might fix things there. One obvious solution is we could start paying decent wages. But according to Paul Doezen, who ran the numbers, this would mean we'd have to charge seven hundred dollars for our high-end iPod instead of three hundred and forty-nine dollars. Bottom line: it's a non-starter. If we're going to make products that people can afford, these products need to be assembled in Chinese sweatshops. And I have to go there to China and see them and feel my soul being fed into a wood-chipper.

"This is the price we pay," Ross Ziehm told me on the plane. "This is the sacrifice that we make so that millions of people might have beautiful objects that restore a sense of childlike wonder to their lives. Is it painful? Yes. Does it harm us? Yes. But we must do this. We must suffer so that others can be happy. It is what we are called to do."

"A guy can only take so much," I say to Mrs. Jobs.

"Just breathe," she says. "Let it out. That's it. Breathe."

29

"I'm slipping," I say. "I can't focus. I can't eat. I can't sleep. Or when I do sleep, I'm having bad dreams. Nightmares."

This is in my shrink's office, in Los Gatos, an emergency visit. It's Saturday night, and he's supposed to be watching his kid in a school play, but I got him to skip that and see me instead. My shrink specializes in treating orphans and adoptees. He does past life regressions, karmic repatterning, soul clearing, and journey-work. Bruce Upstein, Ph.D., is the name on his office door and on his bills, but during our sessions he goes by Linghpra. He's in his late fifties, freakishly thin, and sports a ponytail that reaches halfway down his back.

"Tell me about the nightmares," he says.

We're sitting on pads on the floor, in the lotus position. There's no furniture in the office, just rugs and mats. The walls are hung with Tibetan tapestries. The room is on the seventh floor of an office building, with a glass wall looking out toward the Santa Cruz Mountains.

I tell him about my dream where I'm being crucified next to Bill Gates.

"Actually," he says, "a lot of people have that dream."

"You're kidding."

He shrugs. "Windows users. They hate the guy."

"They should."

"That software takes a toll on people. I see it every day. A lot of people want to see bad things happen to Gates. We see a lot of Windows-related disorders. Post-traumatic stress, that kind of thing."

"But in my dream I'm being crucified too. What's that all about?"

"Separate issue. You're being persecuted. You're being tried for sins that you didn't commit. You might be punished. I suppose you feel like you're being punished already. The bad press, for example. I imagine that's very hurtful."

"It is." I reach for a Kleenex, and wipe my eyes. I'm trying not to cry, but it's not easy.

I tell him about the trip to China, and how it just seems so unfair that I have to go endure that sort of thing.

"I don't know how you do it," he says. "It takes great strength on your part."

"It does," I say. "It saps my energy. It drains me. Then I have to come back here and sit down and try to be creative again. It never lets up. I don't need to be doing this. I could go sit on a beach for the rest of my life. I could be out racing sailboats, like Larry Ellison. I could be running some bogus philanthropy like Bill Gates. But am I? No. Like a fool, I'm still coming in to work every day. I'm still putting in eighteen-hour days. I'm working my ass off. Battling with engineers. Yelling at idiots. Firing people. Getting hassled by everyone. Traveling too much. Never getting enough sleep. Why? Why am I doing this?"

"We've talked about this," Linghpra says. "It's the hole. The hole in your soul, remember?"

"What are you, Doctor fucking Seuss? What's with the rhyming?"

"I'm sorry. You're right." He pauses. He gathers his thoughts. "There's an emptiness," he says. "A vacuum. You try to fill it with work."

"I never should have gone to China. That kid. I can't stop thinking about him. All I want to do is make the world a better place. I have a gift. I want to share it. But it hurts. It physically hurts me. And then I get back here and my own government is attacking me. They're making me out to be a criminal. For what? Because I got paid for my work. Paid well, fair enough. Paid a lot. But look at the value I delivered. Apple's market value has grown sixty billion dollars since I took over. Sixty. Billion. Dollars. I go in every day, I'm doing a thousand things at once, and somehow, okay, maybe somehow, along the way, I made a mistake. *Maybe.* For this they want to put me in jail? After all I've done for the world? Because of a typo? I should be getting the Nobel Prize. Instead they're measuring my neck."

"You're right. It's not fair."

"And do you know what's going to happen? Nobody's going to want to run a public company anymore. Because you can't do the job. Nobody can. You make one slip, you interpret one thing the wrong way, and boom—you're a swindler. You're running a scam. You're lying to shareholders. You're perpetrating a fraud on the American public."

I stop. I take a deep breath and let it out. I roll my neck, trying to release the tension.

"This is good," Linghpra says. "This is good work."

I can't help it. I start to cry.

"Let it out," Linghpra says. "The tears are cleansing."

He leans forward and takes my forearms in his hands. It's an energy flow exercise that we do. You form a circuit and let energy move back and forth between two people, using a form of emotional osmosis. My anger seeps away into him, and his calmness flows into me. He's acting like a radiator, taking the heat from my soul and dissipating it out into the room, returning my energy back to me in a cooler state.

Soon I'm letting go. I begin to sob. Big, heavy, gulping sobs. Linghpra guides me down onto a yoga mat. I lie on my side, with my legs curled up. He lies behind me, cradling me.

"You're a good person," he says.

He pulls himself against me. He holds me tight in his arms and we stay like that for a long time, while he tells me how good I am, and how whatever bad that's happened, it's not my fault.

30

After therapy I go out driving. For hours I roll up and down Route 280 between San Jose and San Francisco, listening to Bob Dylan and trying to clear my head. At about two in the morning I'm heading north in this fantastic section of sweeping turns between Sand Hill Road and Woodside when police lights appear in my rearview mirror and I get pulled over.

It's this total CHPs guy. He's even got the mustache.

"Sir," he says, "do know why I'm standing here?"

"Um, because you couldn't get into college?"

"I'm going to pretend I didn't hear that."

"Oh, *thank you,* officer. I'm so *grateful.* I'm going to recommend that you get a *medal* for your outstanding police work."

I hate cops. Always have. This one informs me that I was going ninety miles per hour. I explain to him that the Mercedes I'm driving has a six-hundred-horsepower engine and can go two hundred miles per hour.

"It's not like I'm in some Volkswagen Golf and I'm gonna blow a gasket or something," I say. "Ninety miles an hour in this car is like standing still. In case you hadn't noticed, there's nobody else out here. The freeway's completely empty."

The guy gets all pissy and wants to see my license. I don't have my license with me. "Do you really not know who I am?"

He tells me to step out of the car.

"Look, sugar tits," I say, "I'm Steve Jobs. I invented the friggin iPod. Have you heard of it?"

Bit of advice here: Do not under any circumstances ever refer to a male highway patrolman as "sugar tits." Next thing I know

I'm flat on the pavement, face down, hands cuffed behind my back. Then I'm in the back of a cruiser and deposited in a lockup in Redwood City.

Also in the cell is some drunk kid who appears to be about seventeen years old and says he works at Kleiner Perkins. He got picked up in his Ferrari on a DUI and has vomited into the sink in the cell. The fascist pigs say they can't clean the sink until tomorrow.

I demand my one phone call. The cop who's running the lockup says the phones aren't working. I tell him I'll use my cell phone. He claims they can't give me my cell phone, for safety reasons.

"You're afraid I'm going to beat myself to death with a cell phone?"

"You'll just have to wait," he says. "Maybe you can spend a little time thinking about what you did wrong."

"I can't believe you just said that."

"Believe what you want."

"You're going to wish you didn't do this to me."

The cop just laughs.

The cell has cement walls, painted gray, with one small window with bars and wire mesh over it. I pop onto the cot in the lotus position and start meditating and humming my syllable. Pretty soon I can barely hear the Kleiner guy moaning. Even the smell of the puke isn't bothering me so much.

At dawn a different cop comes in and asks if we want any breakfast. He says they're making a run to McDonald's. Kleiner Boy orders two Sausage McMuffins, two hash browns, orange juice, and a coffee.

"Is there any chance you could get me a fruit cup?" I say. "Or a smoothie?"

"I'm not a waiter," the cop says. "I'm going to McDonald's. Do you want anything?"

I shake my head. But when the McDonald's food arrives—I'm appalled to say this—the smell of it makes me crazy. Kleiner Boy sees me staring. "You want a bite?" he says.

I shake my head, but I'm still staring. My mouth starts watering. The next time he offers I say okay and he hands me one of the hash brown things. It looks like a scab that came off the back of a horse's balls. But I have to admit, the taste of it—wow. The grease, the cooking fat, the salt. My God. Next thing I know I'm tearing into one of his Sausage McMuffins.

This is the first time I've tasted meat in more than thirty years. In five bites the sandwich is gone. A few seconds later my head is reeling. I lie back on the cot feeling like I'm going to slip into a coma.

I'm lying there fighting to remain conscious when the Apple lawyers arrive, along with Ja'Red. Our lawyers got a call from the captain of the barracks after he came in for his shift and found out who they were holding, and realized he was in deep shit. The lawyers see the McDonald's wrappers on my cot and start freaking out.

"Who did this to you?" one of them says. "Who did this?"

All I can say is, "Ermmm, unnnhhh, oh, I, uh, ermmmm."

One of my guys starts calling for a paramedic. Another starts screaming about Gitmo and the Geneva Convention. Ja'Red, who I'm starting to realize is probably the smartest of the bunch, has the presence of mind to call the Governator. Arnold tells the cops to get me out of the cell immediately, and to go to the captain's office for a conference call.

"I'm ashamed of our state right now," Arnold says. "And you all should be ashamed of yourselves. I hope you are."

"We are," the captain says.

"This person sitting there with you, this is not a regular person," Arnold says. "This guy is a guy that is like a Buddhist monk, do you understand? Like the guy who used to be on the

TV show, the Kung Fu man. You know? A Shaolin priest. This is not a normal human being. This is an enlightened being. Don't the California police get training in how to deal with enlightened beings?"

"We do," the captain says.

"And yet you give him meat? For God's sake!"

"It was a mistake," the captain says. "We're looking into how it happened."

"You must know that you can't do this! A person like this, if you give him meat you could kill him! My God, you could have a dead corpse in that cell right now. There in your lockup. Then how would you be?"

"It was just a Sausage McMuffin," the overnight cop says.

"That's all, eh? Just a Sausage McMuffin? For your information, for this person, for this enlightened being, a Sausage McMuffin is like having a dead rat to be put into his mouth, with the germs and all that. Would you like it if I come up there and put a dead rat in your mouth?"

"No, sir, I wouldn't like that."

"Well that's what you did to this guy, okay? You put a dead rat into his mouth. My God! Steve, I apologize again. If you want to sue the state, I understand, and I'll support you in this."

I tell him no, it's okay, I'd just like to go home.

Arnold tells the pigs that he will be collecting their names and they should stay by their posts and await their new assignments, which will involve things like directing traffic and working construction details. He says if anyone breathes a word of this to the press, he'll have them hung by their nuts.

"Namaste," I tell him. "I bow to your inner Buddha."

"Yeah, same to you and all that," Arnold says.

Outside the sunlight almost knocks me over. The lawyers say I'm barely out of a coma and I should let Ja'Red drive me home. Fair enough. We hop into my car, and I send the lawyers back to headquarters. "Go back to the office and do some work," I say. "Destroy some evidence or something. Find somebody we can sue."

At first I'm glad to be out in the fresh air and looking up at yet another gorgeous California day. But then we get on the 101 and it's a parking lot. We're poking along, starting and stopping, people veering in and out of lanes and beeping their horns, trucks spewing diesel exhaust, Asian kids in their ridiculously souped-up Hondas, this big ugly river of frigtards all going through the motions in their frigtarded lives.

"I can't believe this. This is awful," I say.

"This actually isn't too bad," Ja'Red says. "Most days it's a lot worse than this."

"You're kidding. You sit in traffic like this every day?"

"Most days. Sure."

"Why?"

"To get to work."

"No," I say, "but I mean, why do we do this? What is the point of putting ourselves through this? Not just me and you. But all of mankind. Why do we live this way?"

"Dude," he says, "that's a good question. Seriously. I don't know why."

Mrs. Jobs is waiting in the driveway when we pull up. Ja'Red drops me off and takes my Mercedes to the office.

I try to hug Mrs. Jobs, but she pulls away. "I heard about the meat," she says.

Mrs. Jobs is even stricter about food than I am. It's not just meat. We don't eat candy, or any sugar, or any dairy products. We're completely organic and unprocessed, gluten-free, holistic, macrobiotic. Mostly it's a health thing, but there's also a religious element. It's all about having respect for the planet, and being able to feel a little bit superior to other people. We've even given up fish. Happened to me during the making of *Nemo*. One night I was screening some dailies and it occurred to me that, wow, these are real creatures with real lives. That was it. No way. I couldn't do it anymore. And trust me, I used to *love* sushi.

"You should shower," she says.

I head for the door.

"Not here," she says. "You should go somewhere else. Go to the Four Seasons or something. And you need to get rid of those clothes. Just throw them out. Here."

She hands me a shopping bag with a fresh set of JobsWear: jeans, Issey Miyake black mock turtleneck, sneakers.

"I can smell it on you," she says. "I can smell your sweat. You've got meat sweat. And it's on your breath."

"It's that bad?"

She turns and begins to retch into the bushes.

"You should go to the temple," she says. "You should see the roshi."

"I had a few bites of sausage. That's all."

"That's dead animals," she says. "That's death. You ate death, Steve. You put death into your body."

She starts crying.

"I don't even know who you are anymore," she says.

I look at her. I feel nothing. What kind of monster have I become? I don't know what to say. I walk past her into the house. I go down the hall to my office and lock the door behind me.

She comes down the hall and starts pounding on the door.

"Steve, please!" she says. "Please don't do this!"

"Go away," I tell her.

"It's death!" she says. "Now you've brought it into the house. We'll have to call the roshi. We'll have to have every room repainted. We might have to move."

"Leave me alone."

"Who are you?" She's hysterical now. "Who are you?"

I'm on the floor, curling up into a fetal position, moaning.

"I'm calling Larry," she says. Half an hour later Larry is banging on my door saying if I don't open up and let him in he's going to have his bodyguard come inside and karate chop the door down. Or they'll go to Home Depot and get a circular saw but whatever, they'll get in. So fine, I open the door.

"Holy shit," he says. "What the fuck. You look like shit."

"Nice to see you too."

We sit down. He takes out these incredible buds he's brought back from Hawaii, bright green with red woven through them and totally sticky with resin. We put some Tuvan throat singers on the stereo and do three hits each.

I tell him everything that's been going on. He says he knows this is a shit-sucking period in my life, but there's no way Apple is going to toss me out, and ditto for Disney. And there's no way the feds are going to be allowed to do anything bad to me, he says.

"This is all going to blow over," he says. "You know how these things are. They make all this noise, and then they get tired of it, or bored, or whatever, and they fine you and move on to the next thing. Like I said before, pay them and make this go away."

"It's not just that," I say. "It's the whole thing. The work. Flying back and forth to L.A., going to Asia, never being home.

Or going into Apple and fighting with these bastards over every little detail. I'm tired of it. I'm old."

"You're not old."

"I'm fifty-one. You're sixty-two. You know what the average life expectancy was in Britain in the Middle Ages? Thirty-three years. Guys our age would've been like Gandalf the wizard. If there actually were any guys our age, which I doubt. For damn sure we wouldn't have been working eighteen-hour days, traveling all over the world every week, carrying around all this stress. You know what the life expectancy was at the end of the nineteenth century? Thirty-seven. That was only a hundred years ago."

This is all true. I looked all this stuff up when I had cancer and I was sure I was going to die. I told myself, "Well, even if you do die, you've had a pretty good run."

"You know what you need?" Larry says. "You need an attitude adjustment. Come on over to my place. Hang out for a couple days. We'll do peyote and lie on massage tables while Japanese girls rub our feet."

We really have done this. It's extraordinary. If you ever find yourself with lots of free time and enough money that you can do anything you want, I highly recommend it. But it's not what I need right now.

"I've got to get my focus back. I've lost it. It's like these guys have thrown me. I don't know. This wouldn't have happened before. You know? I wouldn't be so rattled. There's something wrong with me. I'm slipping."

"So take some time off. Take a sabbatical. You want to go hang out in Hawaii? Or Thailand? You remember that time we went to Thailand? Huh?"

I start laughing, because I do remember: Larry got drunk and picked up two girls on Patpong Road and in the morning they turned out to be lady boys, and better yet, they both had the clap. Hilarious.

"Or how about this," he says. "We'll do some prank calls. We can call that idiot Sculley and fuck with his head."

Larry loves to make prank phone calls, especially when he's blitzed. One time he called a hardware store in the Castro and asked them if they had caulk. The guy let out this weary sigh and said yes, in fact, they did have caulk. "And do you have black caulk?" Larry says. "Is it thick? Will it get hard right away and stay hard? Okay, so you do have thick black caulk that will get really, really hard? Cause I need it hard." The guy played along for a while but finally he got sick of it and said, "Girlfriend, do you really think you're the first person who's ever called here asking for caulk? Do you really think that's original? And, by the way, Mr. Lawrence Ellison, you might want to turn off your caller ID before you make prank calls, okay? Have a nice day!"

But even that didn't stop Larry. He fixed the caller ID and called a Thai restaurant in Mountain View and asked them if they had chicken satay, and did it come with penis sauce? What kind of penis? Was it Asian penis? What did the penis sauce taste like? Was it salty?

But the calls to old Agent Sculley are the best. I know it's probably childish of me to still be so angry over something that happened more than twenty years ago. But I'm sorry. I recruited the guy to help run Apple. I trusted him. I considered him a friend. Then he goes behind my back and gets me tossed out of my own company. He's lucky all I do is prank call him.

We've been doing this for years. Every time we get him he changes his phone number. But we always manage to get the new one and sting him again. We'll wake him up at three in the morning and ask him if he's got Prince Albert in a can, or I'll tell him I'm a telemarketer raising money for the Unemployed CEO Foundation. Or I'll do the one where I pretend I work for the phone company and I say I'm down at the end of his street and please don't pick up the phone because if you do I'll get shocked, and then I call back and when he picks up I scream like I'm being shocked and I go, "Ow! Ow! Ouch! Hey! Bzzzzzt! Bzzzzzt! Hey! I told you not to pick up the phoooooone!!! G-g-g-g-g-g . . . aaaaaaaarghhhhh!!!"

But the best one ever, the one where we really got him, was when I called him one night right after dinner and asked him if he would come talk to us about running Apple again.

"I know we've had our differences," I say, "but I'm so busy with the Pixar and Disney stuff, I can't do both jobs, I'm burning out, blah blah, and we really need you, I'm begging you, please, just come in and talk to the board, we're meeting tomorrow, so just hear what we have to say."

The poor suffering idiot hasn't had a real job since Apple tossed him out in 1993. So of course he falls for it and comes bounding in the next day all dressed up in his snazzy suit for his big comeback moment, like he's probably been up all night jizzing all over himself just thinking about being CEO of Apple again.

Only when he gets to the lobby our receptionist tells him that nobody is expecting him, and there's no board meeting. She says she's never even heard of him. He pushes back, and so she calls for her supervisor.

"There's a Mr. Scalley here," she says.

Security arrives. They say there must be some mix-up. They tell Sculley I'm not even on the campus, I'm in China. Really I'm up in the Jobs Pod with Larry and Lars Aki, and we're watching the whole thing and laughing our asses off. Sculley knew it, too. For a long time he just stood there in the lobby staring up at the security camera. Then he gave us the finger and stomped out. We switched to the camera feed from the parking lot and saw him slumped in his Mercedes, staring into space. Priceless.

"Or how about that guy from Pixar?" Larry says. "Remember? The IT guy? The guy who wanted to be CEO?"

This was back when I had just rejoined Apple and they hadn't named me CEO yet. Officially we were doing a job search for that position. This guy, who knew me at Pixar and kind of had a few screws loose, published this long open letter to me on his website, saying he wanted to apply for the job and listing all the things Apple needed to do to get back in shape again.

So Larry and I called him and told him he had the job. The poor bastard called the *San Jose Mercury News* and told them he'd been hired to be the CEO of Apple. Then the Merc and all these other newspapers did stories about how this guy had been hoaxed.

"You know what?" Larry says. "I bet you a thousand bucks that if we call that guy up right now, we could get him to fall for it again. Can you imagine? So where is that guy anyway? You still got his phone number?"

"You know," I say, "I heard that guy committed suicide."

"You're shitting me. Jesus. Well, that fucks up everything, doesn't it? Okay, so let's find someone else."

I tell him I can't really get into any of this right now. But Larry likes to believe he's the world's greatest salesman, so he's not going to give up that easily. He says, "I've got it. We'll have one of those fake Pixar movie premier parties. We'll do it up in San Francisco again, and invite all the chiptards from the Valley and put out a red carpet and the klieg lights and the whole deal. We'll all put on tuxedos, and we'll hire a bunch of fake paparazzi and some fake autograph hounds. Remember McNealy walking in on the last one, thinking the whole thing was for real, like there actually were people who were dying for his autograph? Brother, that was rich."

"Larry," I say, "are we bad people? Are we evil?"

"What?"

"Are we evil?"

"Who? You and me?"

"All of us," I say.

"Are you crazy? Of course not. We're not evil. We're the good guys. We've made the world a better place. That's why we're rich."

"You really believe that?"

"Yes," he says. "I really do."

"How have we made the world a better place?"

"Well, just for one thing, what about the iPod," he says. "Look what that's done. People can carry their music collection with them wherever they go."

"The iPod," I say, "is just a way for the music companies to get people to buy the same recordings all over again. For the third time. First the LP, then the CD, now the iPod. Come on. You know that."

"Well you're making money at it," he says.

"Yup." I sigh. "I'm making money." I sit there, staring at the wall.

"What?"

"Nothing."

"Oh, now don't start on the money stuff. You're not going to go shave your head again, are you?"

"I'm fine."

"So let's do it. We'll have a movie party. We can send out invitations tomorrow. We'll even rent a couple of actors to add some sex appeal. How much is Nick Nolte going for these days? Or Melody Bishop? I'm pretty sure I screwed her once, so maybe I get a discount. At least I think I screwed her. Is she the one with the blonde hair and the big fat collagen lips?"

"We don't have any new movies coming out."

"So we'll call it a DVD release party. A director's cut of *Nemo,* with some bonus crap on the disk."

"We've got none of those coming out either."

"Who cares if you actually have a product to sell? Doesn't mean you can't have a release party. We do this all the time at Oracle. It's called marketing, buddy. Can't believe I have to explain this to you, of all people. Look, Steve, you know what? I'll even pay for it. Just to get out of the house and have some fun. Whatever."

This time I can't even answer. I'm sitting there, stoned out of my head, mesmerized by the screen saver on my computer.

Larry snaps his fingers in front of my face.

"Jobso," he says.

"What."

"No more eating meat. Okay?"

"Okay."

After he's gone I call Breezeann on the intercom and tell her to bring me a mango smoothie. It helps. In the afternoon I meet Kuso Sukatoro at the Apple building for a double-duty colonic to flush out the toxins from the meat.

"You feel better now?" she asks, as she's putting her equipment away.

"I do," I say, but I'm not sure if I'm telling the truth.

At any given moment the San Jose Jet Center probably has more rich people walking around under its roof than any other building on earth. This is where everyone in the Valley keeps their private jets, and like all of the old-school Valley locations it remains intentionally drab, with crappy furniture and worn-out carpeting and faded paint. Old-money guys in the Valley—by which I mean anyone who's been rich since before the Internet bubble of the late nineties—totally get off on shabbiness. They might ski in Utah, but not at Deer Valley. That's for new money people, like Google employees and Web 2.0 strivers. The old guys ski at Alta.

So a crappy jet terminal with shitty instant coffee in styrofoam cups is just perfect. That may be because it helps us forget that we're flying around in planes that cost ten thousand dollars per hour to operate. The other reason that nobody cares about how bad this terminal looks, of course, is that nobody ever sits around here. People like me don't wait for flights. Our planes wait for us. We show up and go.

Except today. Today it is raining. I mean *raining*. The drops are as big as grapes, and they're falling so hard they're carving divots in the grass. It's noon, and the sky is pitch black. Sheet lightning keeps blasting out of the Santa Cruz Mountains. Trees are bending sideways in the wind. They look as if they might rip up out of the ground and fly away.

So we're stuck, maybe fifty of us, waiting for the storm to blow over, when in walk three FBI agents and a bunch of uniformed San Jose cops. Right behind them is a crew from KSJT, the local TV station.

The cops go up to Sanjay Dash, the CEO of Altona Semiconductor, and three of his executives, and start reading them their rights. Handcuffs, the whole thing. The FBI guys make a big show, I suppose to be sure that all the rest of us see what's happening. They perp walk the guys out to a van and haul them away. When they're gone the TV idiots come back inside and try to get interviews. The reporter is a woman in her twenties with blonde hair, a black suit and sneakers. She rushes around shoving her microphone at people. Nobody will talk to her. She tapes a spot anyway, and makes it seem as if Sanjay and his guys were arrested while trying to flee the country, which is apparently what the FBI guys told her. Nice touch.

It's the third big arrest in less than a week. Nick Malone of MTware and Dave Tsao of Mantis Networks were perp-walked out of their offices. Mark Broder of Xictel, a chip company, was picked up at Bentley's in Woodside, leaving his wife sobbing into her duck confit and *pommes salardaise*.

"It's not going to stop," Misho Knedlik says. "Now that there's blood in the water, there'll be more, not less. Trust me, this was how it happened in Bratislava, back in the Communist days. In Bratislava it was always at the train station. So everyone could see you being humiliated. It sends a message: You could be next. Scares the shit out of people. Look at this place."

He's right. People are freaking out. Most of them are on their cell phones, looking frantic. A few are just sitting down, staring out at the rain, looking scared and dumbfounded. Larry and I and Misho are sharing a green plastic table beside a window overlooking the runway.

"I'll tell you what, I'm glad I'm retired," Misho says.

"So's everyone else," Larry says.

Misho is the former CEO of Bronson Microelectronics. He's seventy-five years old, a trim little Jewish dude with curly hair and twinkly eyes that almost make you forget what a monster he was to everyone who ever worked for him—or did business with him, or bought products from him, or, God forbid, tried to compete against him. He's a Slovak who escaped from Czechoslovakia in the fifties with the clothes on his back, got a Ph.D. in engineering, joined a semiconductor company, worked his way up to CEO, and got rich. Then he invested in a venture fund and got ten times richer.

Misho is nowhere near being rich the way Larry and I are rich, but he's done well enough. He's also the rudest person in the Valley and definitely the most hated, ever since he published a memoir called *Everyone Wants to Kill You,* which managed to offend pretty much everyone in the industry. Larry was one of the guys who got stung the worst by the things Misho said about him. Not that they weren't true; they were. Everyone out here knew the stories. Still, nobody had ever dared put them in print.

"They'll be after you next," Misho says, meaning me.

I just shrug. He's probably right, but I don't want to let on that I'm scared.

"You know what I'd do if I were in your shoes?" he says. "I'd walk out. The way they're treating you? Come on. Let some other asshole run the company. Besides, how many more years you think you're going to live? Go spend those years with your kids. Move to Maui. Spend your days on the beach."

"I'd last about a month," I say, "before I'd go nuts."

"Why, you think what you do here matters? You think it's important? Who gives a shit about computers? I wish I'd bought my place in Hawaii twenty years ago."

"He's right," Larry says. "I'm thinking about retiring myself."

"You? Retire?" Misho bursts out laughing. "Retire from what? Sailing? Fucking interns? When was the last time you showed up at the office three days in a row and put in a full eight hours? *You're* gonna retire? Who could even tell? You lazy cocksucker."

Misho takes a sip of his coffee and spits it out onto the floor.

"What the fuck is this," he says.

"Nescafé," Larry says, "and Coffee-mate. It's all they've got. I put in two sugars."

"I'd rather drink hemlock."

"Let me go see if they have some." Larry heads off to the men's room.

"Why do you hang around with that asshole?" Misho says.

"He's a good guy."

"No he's not. So tell me. You had any shareholder suits yet?"

"Five so far. More coming, I'm told."

"Bloodsuckers. Your stock's done what? Tripled since you took over?"

"Quadrupled. Whatever. We'll settle the cases."

"You know how I'd settle them?" Misho says. "A bullet in the back of the head. Fucking lawyers."

He turns to the window. It's raining even harder now.

"Look at this shit," he says. "We're never gonna get out of this shithole. I hate this place. This whole fucking Valley. I hate it. It's changed. It used to be a good place. Now it's just shit. Just scammers. Idiots trying to make a buck."

33

"**I found a janitor,**" Larry says when he returns. "He says they don't have hemlock, but they do have some rat poison if you want to eat that instead."

"I'll think about it," Misho says.

Larry stands at the window watching the rain bucketing down. "Only time I've seen rain like this was during the monsoon season in Nam," he says,

"You were in Vietnam?"

"Oh yeah."

"What were you? Marines?"

"Oh, not the war," Larry says. "Vacation. Bunch of times. Beautiful place. Amazing women. You can order them by the dozen. Incredible."

"Oy." Misho makes a big deal out of being repulsed by Larry. I'm never sure if it's an act or if he really hates him. But

Misho has been married to the same woman for fifty years, so I'm guessing Larry pretty much makes him sick.

The other thing that makes Misho sick is Communism, and it's also one of his favorite subjects, and now that he's got his teeth into it he can't let go.

"They used to come through the neighborhood and round people up," he says. "You'd get a knock at the door in the middle of the night. They'd take your house, your land. *Liberation,* they called it. They'd liberated you from your property. Oh, and *freedom.* That was their big cause. All it meant was they were free to take your stuff."

He goes on about army camps and gulags, and I'm trying to pay attention, but Larry keeps leaning back on the couch making yap-yap-yap gestures with his hand and twirling his index finger in little circles beside his head.

Fair enough. We've all heard Misho's stories a million times. And yes, they're boring. But the thing is, I kind of love Misho. I can't bring myself to be rude to him. Larry is now miming a blowjob, jamming his fist toward his open mouth and poking his tongue against his cheek. Then he starts pretending to hang himself, tugging at an invisible noose around his neck and sticking out his tongue.

"That's what this country is coming to," Misho says. "These rules. This Sarbanes-Oxley bullshit. What is this? They're making it a crime to run a company. Whose great idea was this?"

"It's an epidemic," Larry says. "It's like AIDS, back in the early eighties, back when nobody knew what caused it."

"I bet you were scared shitless back then, weren't you? Mr. Gay Guy."

"What are you talking about?"

"I'm sure you've been gay. You've got that look. You've got the gay eyes."

"Misho, do you have Alzheimer's? Have you been checked?"

"Those big eyelashes. Very effeminate. That's how you can tell a gay, did you know that, Steve? The eyes. Plus, the guy's had a fucking facelift, for Christ's sake."

"Two face lifts," I say. "And two eye jobs."

"What straight man gets a face lift? And you wear makeup."

"That was one time," Larry says, "and I'd just been on NBC. I came straight from the studio."

"Maybe you came from the studio, but not *straight*," Misho says. He turns to me. "Guy shows up at Chantilly looking like a drag queen. The waiters were jumping into his lap. And don't tell me you have to wear makeup on TV. I've done plenty of TV. They want to talk to me, fine, bring in the camera and turn it on and start asking questions. You don't like how I look? Fuck you. Don't do the interview. They tried putting that shit on me once and I told the guy, 'Get away from me or I'll stab you in the eye with your makeup brush, you fruitcake.'"

"Steve wears makeup," Larry says. "When he's on stage. Giving speeches."

"It's not makeup," I say. "It's a base layer. More like a moisturizer."

"Jesus, the two of you." Misho shakes his head. "You know, it used to be *men* out here. Engineers. You had to know something. Now it's fags like you. No education, no training. Over at HP they had those two broads running the place. What the fuck was that, can you tell me?"

"Always uplifting to hang out with you, Misho," Larry says. "A real pleasure. Total edification. Thanks."

"You're welcome." Misho lifts his ass cheek and farts in Larry's direction. He looks across the lobby at Larry Page and Sergey Brin from Google. "And don't even get me started on those idiots."

The Google guys are here with a bunch of SOMA-type guys from Web 2.0 social networking and video-sharing companies— zippr, zaggl, I can never remember—and a busload of college girls. They're whooping it up, passing around a bottle of tequila and shouting, "Vegas, baby!" which is I guess where they're going on the Google jumbo jet. The guys are wearing T-shirts and ripped-up jeans, and they've got those haircuts where you pay two hundred bucks to make it look like you just got out of bed.

"All the money they've got, it would kill them to go buy some decent clothes? And maybe shave in the morning? Bunch of bums. In the old days there was a certain standard."

Misho isn't the only one who hates these guys. None of the old-school guys can stand what's happened to the Valley since the Internet was created.

"I can't believe I'm saying this," Larry says, "but for once I actually agree with you. This stuff these kids are making, a monkey could do it. Try writing an enterprise database program. Fifteen million lines of code."

"Try designing a microprocessor," Misho says. "Try investing five billion dollars every time you need to build a new wafer fab. You gotta have balls like a gorilla," he says, grabbing his crotch, "to be in the chip business."

"You know what? It's over," Larry says. "The computer business, the chip business, the software business. We did it, it was fun, we all got rich, but it's over. I'm putting my money into biotech. Anti-aging products. Life extenders. We've got this huge generation of boomers who suddenly realize they're gonna get old and die, and guess what. They're not thrilled about this. Next big boom is going to be bioengineering, stuff that will let you live to be a hundred and forty."

"I can barely stand being seventy-five," Misho says. "I look in the mirror after my shower and I disgust myself."

"I'm talking about being a hundred years old and looking like you're fifty," Larry says. "And a *good* fifty. You're telling me you wouldn't spend a million bucks to live another seventy years?"

"I'd spend a million to make sure it doesn't happen. I'd spend two million to make doubly sure it doesn't happen to you. No sir. No thank you." Misho turns to me. "Let me tell you something. You and I are not going to live to be a hundred years old. And we both know the one thing that money can't buy. Time. Every day it's ticking down. Tick, tick, tick."

Larry starts playing an invisible violin. Misho ignores him.

"Twenty years ago I missed my daughter's high-school graduation. You know why? I was in Taiwan, beating the shit out of some equipment supplier. Told myself it was real important. Right. My daughter's grown up now. She's got kids. To this day she holds it against me. You know how much I'd pay to get that day back?"

"I hear what you're saying."

"Then do something about it. Before these assholes from the government start tearing you to pieces."

"I'll tell you what we're gonna do," Larry says. "We're going to organize a war council. We're going to start calling in favors from these assholes in Washington who've been taking our money and doing nothing for us. I'm going to call Bill."

Larry gave Bill Clinton twenty million dollars over the course of his presidency, and ten million more for his library after he left office.

"Fantastic," Misho says. "Another guy who can't keep his dick in his pants. You two must get along great. How do you lure him out here? Tell him you found a new glory hole up in the Castro?"

"That's it exactly," Larry says.

"Well, ladies." Misho slaps his knees and stands up. "It's been a pleasure. But I'm leaving. I promise I'll come visit you in prison. Or I'll pay someone to do it for me, probably. Okay? Good luck to you."

So Larry actually manages to put together a war council. He sets it up at John Doerr's house in Woodside, because Doerr is tight with Bill Clinton these days and supposedly he's angling to get some cabinet post in a Hillary administration.

I arrive late, because to hell with getting anywhere early and sitting around waiting. The house looks like some drug lord's palace from a Chuck Norris movie, with a bunch of black armored SUVs and—I swear to God—a helicopter hovering overhead. They've got snipers on the roof, and a bunch of ape-looking guys with the earbuds standing out front. I've been to enough of these things to know what Secret Service agents look like. I'm pretty sure the show is Larry's doing, because he gets off on the whole James Bond effect.

The gorillas frisk me and find a lighter in my jeans. They tell me I'll have to leave it with them and pick it up on the way out and I say, "Well, there goes my plan to torch the place, but whatever."

I go inside and there's little Doerr, all ninety-seven pounds of him, with his too-big eyeglasses and his freako metabolism and the usual stick up his ass. He takes me to this room where all the big-shots from the Valley are sitting around a table. It's like the meeting of the Five Families scene from Godfather One. There's

Otellini and Ruiz and T.J. Rodgers and some other chip guys, plus the Googletards who are playing with Legos, and McNealy, Schwartz, Hurd, Barksdale, Andreesen, Chambers, Barksdale, plus the money guys like Khosla and Jurvetson and McNamee and a bunch of other random VC assholes. Then there are a dozen or so guys I sort of kind of recognize from conferences, guys who work for second-tier outfits.

I figure there's two hundred billion dollars sitting in this room. That's just personal net worth. If you added up the market value of the companies these guys control, you're talking close to a trillion. They're all sitting around with notepads in front of them, expecting, I guess, to make big speeches.

In walk the Clintstones with George Soros. No smiles, no small talk. Hillary sits down and tells us in this pissed off Tony Soprano voice that there's two years till this motherfucking election but she isn't gonna fuck it up like Kerry and Gore, she's gonna lock this motherfucker down now, she's goddamn well gonna win and nobody is gonna get in her way, so we can all either get on the train or get run over by it, and she's here to tell us how much money she wants each of us to put in.

Larry butts in and says that we'd arranged this meeting hoping to discuss ways in which we might put an end to the persecution and witch hunt that is currently taking place in the Valley. He's smooth enough not to mention words like "coup" and "assassination," but Hillary gives him this withering look anyway and says, "If you don't mind, Barry, I'd like to continue."

Larry looks at Bill, and in a voice that's pretty controlled, considering that he's given these people thirty million dollars over the years, he says, "Um, did we get our wires crossed here or something?"

Bill gives him this battered spouse look, as if to say, *Hell, brother, don't get me into hot water here, okay? Ix-nay on the alking-tay.*

"Excuse me, Bill's not running this meeting," Hillary says, and then she starts in again, saying everybody else pays their share, the oil guys pay five percent of net right off the top, and meanwhile we're out here making our little chips and paying whatever we feel like, which for some of us, too many of us in fact, is zero.

"That bullshit," she says, "is gonna stop. Right here and now."

She tells us we can all check with George Soros on the way out and he'll tell us how to move the money so it can't be traced, using a bunch of these phony baloney environmental groups. She goes right around the table and gives everyone their number and what they'll get if they do or don't play ball.

Doerr gets oil prices bumped to a hundred bucks a gallon so his green tech fund can pop out a few winners. The Googletards get net neutrality so they can keep abusing copyright and selling ads against other people's content. McNealy can sell his over-priced Sun boxes to government agencies, and Hillary will lift some export restrictions so he can sell supercomputers to the North Koreans. McNealy says he'd also like a fresh DOJ case on Microsoft, but Hillary says no can do because Gates is putting up half a billion to buy a free pass.

In my case the nut is twenty million dollars, and if I go along, the SEC and U.S. Attorney drop the charges on the options stuff and the feds buy iMacs for every school system in America. If I don't, the options hassle continues, plus the DOJ will join with the Europeans who are raping us over the iPod being a closed system.

"Ya know, Steve," she says, "the Euros ain't the only ones who can bend you over and stick it up your ass."

So I kind of laugh and go, "Well, ma'am, I appreciate your offer to help us out, but the thing is, with some of this stuff, like the options witch hunt, well, we need some help on this stuff right now, you see? We can't really wait until 2008. Also, the thing is, I'm planning to endorse Al Gore, if he runs, because he's on my board, and he's going to save the planet from melting, and he's going to make my pal Bono the head of the Supreme Court or something."

She stares at me with this flabbergasted look, as if she can't believe that someone else actually dared to speak instead of genuflecting and doing whatever she tells them, which is I guess what most people do around her.

Then she says, in that stupid chipmunk voice of hers, "You know, I really didn't come here for a dialogue, I just wanted to give you information and leave, but since you raised the issue, let me reassure you, the world isn't melting, Steve. Honestly. Al made that movie to scare people. Although if you want to know what's really scary it's the prospect of having that hillbilly in the White House. Do you know how much of a mess he made during our time there? Do you have any idea what it was like to be constantly stamping out his stupid ideas! I mean Kyoto? Fuck me, seriously.

"You do realize that Al has been in and out of psychiatric hospitals, right? They keep him medicated beyond belief. That's why he talks like that. Every so often he'll go off his meds and cook up some stupid idea. Whenever he did, the rest of us would all have to go racing around to find his shrink and get him shot up with something or other and put back in his straitjacket."

"Well," I say, "if Al doesn't run, then I'm probably going for Jerry Brown. Or Ralph Nader. Or maybe Obama."

"Stevie, honey, you can endorse Osama bin Laden for all I care. You can go stand on a street corner wearing a fucking sandwich board and dance around in your tighty-whities. I just want your *money*, sweetie. It's really simple. If you pay up, I help you. If you don't, I won't. Okay? By the way, what is up with those hippie eyeglasses? There's these things called contact lenses now, have you heard of them?"

Now I'm the one who's stunned. Nobody makes fun of my John Lennon glasses. Nobody. Seriously.

For a long time I just sit there, staring down at my hands, trying to stay calm. Doerr, who knows how I feel about my glasses, says, "Steve, whatever you're thinking, just let it go, okay? Let it go."

But I can't help myself. I go, "Lady, let me tell you something. I grew up in this Valley, okay? And nobody comes into our Valley and talks to us like this. You see the guys in this room? We're guys who build things. All right, with the exception of the VCs, who are parasites. But I'm talking about the rest of us. We're engineers. We're the guys who built the friggin Internet, with our bare hands. Do you understand? Me personally, I've been through hell and back. I've been fired from my own company. I've survived cancer. Then I invented the friggin iPod. I'm not scared of you. Let's get something straight. I've got five billion dollars. If you want some of that, you come here and you *ask* me. Not *tell* me. You *ask*. You kiss the ring, just like your husband and everybody else. You got that straight?"

"Well," she says, "that was a lovely speech. You know in Washington we have this thing called etiquette. Have you heard of it?"

"You know," I say, "in California we have this thing called Pilates. Have you heard of it? You should check it out, because let me tell you, you've got a really big fat lumpy ass. I mean you can't even tell if there's actually an ass in there. It's like two big garbage bags full of oatmeal. Seriously."

Her face starts to shake. Beside her, I swear, Bill is working very hard at not laughing. The rest of the room is silent.

Finally, way down at the far end of the table, T.J. Rodgers stands up and starts doing a slow clap. Some others join in. Soon the whole room is clapping and shouting, *Steve, Steve, Steve—*

except for Doerr, who's all bummed out because his Secretary of State job just went up in smoke.

The Clintstones and Soros make for the door, with Doerr scrambling after them apologizing and begging them not to leave, but Hillary says, "Fuck you, gerbil, don't call me ever again," and she throws us all the finger. We all roar laughing and give her the finger right back. Ha! Thanks for coming to California, lady. Come back anytime!

We all file out past Doerr, who is standing in his foyer looking all shattered because he really, really wants to be a cabinet member. Doerr gives us this fake little smile and says, "Thanks for coming, guys. Great seeing you, as always."

When I got to my car, no lie, somebody has keyed my door. I know it was one of the Clintons. Probably Hillary. Fat ass.

35

I'm less than a mile down the road when my cell phone rings. It's Tom Bowditch. He's already heard what happened.

"Kid," he says, "you are your own worst enemy. You know that? You've actually managed to make things worse."

In the background there's music playing. Girls are shrieking, and someone is shouting in Russian.

"Where are you?" I say.

"The Black Sea. Place called Sochi. On my boat." The vehicle which Tom calls a boat is a three-hundred-foot-long mega-yacht that cost him a hundred million dollars. It attracts Russian hookers like light bulbs attract moths.

"You need a lawyer," he says. "I've got one for you."

It's a guy in New York who represented a bunch of investment bankers and analysts who got in trouble after the dotcom crash. He also consulted on the Martha Stewart case and for some of the Enron guys. And he does a lot of work for the Mob, but only on the high-end cases and always behind the scenes.

"Trust me," Tom says, "this guy is the best. He did the John Gotti case. Donald Trump keeps him on permanent retainer just to handle sexual harassment cases."

"I'm surprised he has time to do anything else."

"You and me both. Look, get ready to spend some money, because this guy costs a fortune. But when I tell you this guy's the best, I mean he's pure evil. And tough. Grew up in the Bronx. This guy could fuck a bag of broken glass and make it cry."

"I'll be sure to bring one with me when I meet him."

"He's coming to you. I sent my jet to get him. He'll come to your house, not the office. He's a freak about secrecy. Okay? Don't say I never did you a favor."

Bobby DiMarco is the guy's name and yes, it's *Bobby*, not Robert or Bob. *Bobby.* "Or some people call me *Bobby D*," he says, and he's one of those guys who shakes your hand and keeps pumping it and doesn't let go. Hoo boy.

He's in his late forties, about five-foot-five, and appears to be almost as wide as he is tall, with jet-black hair combed back from his face and a big brush mustache that makes him look like Geraldo Rivera. He's wearing a navy blue suit which appears to be very expensive, and some very strong cologne. He's carrying an aluminum briefcase with a lock on it.

Mr. Joebs, he calls me. With a long "o." Which is one of my pet peeves. I mean, could I be any more in the public eye? Are there really still people who don't know how to pronounce my name? Really? And if this guy is so good how come he hasn't even bothered to check this out?

I explain it to him nicely. "It's *Jobs*," I say. "Rhymes with knobs."

"Okay," he says. "Okay. Great."

Fair enough. I don't like him. Who says I need to like the guy? I ask him my usual job applicant questions, like, "How many times have you done LSD?" and "When did you lose your virginity?"

"Pass," he says. "Now listen. I've looked over everything, and I hate to tell you, but honestly, the government does have a case here. Not a big case, but a case. Enough to indict anyway."

He goes on to tell me how things will work, which is that, just like in the Martha Stewart case, they'll bring me in and ask me loads of questions and try to get me to lie.

"It's called a perjury trap," he says. "Martha fell for it. But don't worry. I'm going to be with you. We're not going to walk into that. Martha's big mistake was she went in there without a lawyer thinking she could talk to these assholes like they're human beings. Know this right now. These are not human beings. And this is not about justice. This is about savage motherfuckers—excuse my French, I'm sorry—savage predators who want to make a name by taking you down. I know, because I used to be one of them. You ever watch these shows on the nature channels, out on the Serengeti or whatever? With the predator and the prey? It's like that. It's not because it's right or wrong. It's not about the law, or justice. These guys are predators. They've decided to hunt you. Okay? Are we straight on this?"

"This meeting isn't doing a lot for my mood," I tell him.

"Hey, look, you should be smiling! We can do way better than Martha. She did five months in and five months with a bracelet. The worst we're going to do is one or the other. Five at home with a bracelet, or five inside and no bracelet."

"Wow. Only five months? Well now I feel great. How much are you charging me?"

"It's like I tell Tom. You want someone to tickle your asshole with a feather, hire Richard Simmons, or go talk to those cheerleaders you got working on your legal team at Apple. You want the truth, call me."

He says we should definitely put off meeting Doyle for as long as possible, and whatever I do, I should never sit down with Doyle or talk to anyone from his office unless I've got DiMarco and about fifty other lawyers with me. I tell him Doyle looks to me like a complete frigtard and he says, "No, see, that's where you're wrong. Doyle is a very, very smart guy. And this kid he's got working for him, this William Poon? Scary smart. And fucking vicious."

"Maybe you hadn't noticed," I say, "but I'm pretty smart myself."

He coughs into his hand and says we should move on and discuss strategy. He starts to explain his plan of action but I cut him off and tell him I've already figured out the strategy.

"First off, we admit Sonya and Zack actually did something funky, and maybe they deserve to go to jail. But what does any of this have to do with me? You see? Where's the connection? I don't see it. Yes, they gave the options to me. If anything, that makes me the victim. They dragged me into this. Right? I didn't put my name on any documents. *They* did."

"Well," he says, "I like the way you're thinking here."

"So can we run with this?"

"Um, no."

"What?"

"Look, it's complicated. Anyway, the point is, anything that happens from now on, you let me deal with it. Okay? You don't say anything. No more meetings with Sampson. Definitely no meetings with the feds. You got it? Unless I look it over first and set the ground rules and sit there with you."

He gets up to leave.

"You know what else I don't get?" I say.

"What's that."

"Bill Gates foists Windows off on the world, and he remains a free man. I give the world OS X, the iMac, and the friggin iPod. I save Apple from what looked like certain death. I make billions for our shareholders. Now they want to throw me in prison and throw away the key. What's up with that?"

"Hey," he says, "I'm a lawyer, not a shrink, all right? Here." He hands me his card. "There's a cell number on the back, in red. That's my private line. Call me any time you want, day or night. Doesn't matter what time it is. And like I said, zip the lip."

Next morning I arrive at the Jobs Pod and there on my desk— the big one, the one with nothing on it— someone has placed a copy of the *Wall Street Journal*. Ja'Red swears he has no idea how it got onto my desk. "It was there when I got in," he says.

The paper has been taken apart so that the B section is on top. Right on page B1 they've got one of their cheesy little line drawings of my own chief operating officer, Jim Bell. There's also a huge profile, which fills the entire right-hand column of B1, and a full jump page describing what a wonderful, smart, professional guy Jim Bell is, telling all about his childhood in

Mississippi and where he went to college and how he was *summa cum laude* at Ole Miss and first in his class at Stanford Business School. Man.

In case you don't know what it means to have your company's Number Two guy glowingly profiled on B1 of the *Wall Street Journal,* let me explain it to you: someone is trying to kill me. And I'm pretty sure I know who it is.

This maneuver is classic Tom Bowditch, using the press to tee up his new CEO. You can tell it's Tom because with Tom it's always the *Journal.* Not the *Times.* Tom hates the *Times,* thinks they're too liberal. But he's got friends at the *Journal.* He feeds them dirt on companies, and in return, when he needs a favor, he picks up the phone. He'll put a bug in the ear of some editor at the *Journal,* who passes word to some other editor, and next thing you know it's getting mentioned to a reporter, and it's all so smooth that this poor sap reporter who wrote the article probably believes he thought it up himself.

Basically, Tom is the devil. I've always known that. I just thought that he was my devil. Wrong, apparently. The other reason I know he's involved is because I know Jim Bell wouldn't have the balls to try to stab me in the back on his own.

So what can I do? I call Jim, ostensibly to congratulate him. My call goes through to voice mail. I try Tom. Suddenly he's not picking up either. So I leave him a voice mail saying, "I know this is your work, asshole. I've seen you in operation, doing this very same thing when you were on the board at Ford, remember?"

Of course Tom isn't quoted in the story or even mentioned by name. Neither is Jim Bell. They make a big point of saying that Jim Bell wouldn't speak to the reporter. Same for Apple. A company spokesman declined to comment.

So let's think about this. One day, for no good reason, and with no cooperation from Apple, the *Journal* just decided to profile some executive at Apple that nobody has ever heard of before. Really. Wow. Plus the story is loaded up with a bunch of flattering quotes and anecdotes from Jim's friends. You think those people spoke to the *Journal* without Jim's permission? Please.

But I must admit, whoever put this together did a splendid job. It's one of those stories where the real message is located between the lines, and you need to decode it. It's aimed directly at the guys on Wall Street. And the not-so-hidden message is, "Don't worry, even if Jobs goes to jail, the company will be fine. There's no reason to dump the stock."

Some examples:

1. Jim Bell is a quiet and soft-spoken guy who stays out of the limelight but is largely responsible for keeping the company running. Translation: He's already running the place.

2. When Steve Jobs had cancer a couple years ago, Jim Bell was in charge of the company. Translation: Don't worry, we're fine without El Jobso.

3. Jim Bell often receives inquiries from recruiters who want him to become CEO of some other company. Translation: He's CEO material, and he'll be great here.

4. Jim Bell has no connection to the mess with stock options. Translation: He's clean, and ethical, unlike that son of a bitch Steve Jobs.

The article contains a few anecdotes about how old Jim straightened up our manufacturing processes and how everyone likes him. He's smart and analytical and detail-oriented, and a courtly Southern gentleman to boot, as opposed to yours truly, who's described as having a "mercurial temper and sharp tongue" and who "recently fired Apple's legendary head of engineering, Michael Dinsmore, a move that alienated many inside the company."

Bottom line: a coup is brewing. There's a mutiny in the ranks, a battle for control of the company. It's like that movie where the babysitter is getting these creepy phone calls so she calls the phone company and the operator says the creepy calls are coming from inside the house.

How long until the mutineers make their move? I give myself a month, tops. Any day now the phone will ring and it'll be Tom Bowditch telling me we have a special board meeting. Next thing you know I'll be sipping margaritas with Carly Fiorina and Scott McNealy at some support group meeting for washed-up CEOs at Bennigan's in Santa Clara. Maybe I can take up Segway polo with Woz. Or spend some of my money and get myself shot up into space, like all the other billionaires who don't know what to do with themselves. Damn.

When I finally do reach Tom Bowditch he doesn't even bother trying to deny it. "Kid," he says, "we're trying to cover our asses here, okay? This isn't personal. It's business. And this Dinsmore thing, kid, it's serious. I'm urging you to seriously reconsider. At a time like this, to be firing key people? Think how it looks. And if you're not careful you're going to have a mutiny on your hands down there in the engineering labs."

I try to seem cool. I tell Tom that I appreciate his position and that I'll be happy to step aside if he thinks that's what's best for the company.

"I just hope you and the rest of the board remember what this company looked like before I came back," I say.

"We all know how important you are to the company."

"Important? I'm *Steve Jobs*."

"That's right." He sighs. "You're Steve Jobs."

"I invented the friggin iPod. Have you heard of it?"

He says that yes, he's heard of the iPod. I tell him that maybe he thinks I'm a pushover because the last time they kicked me out I put my tail between my legs and split. Well, not this time. This time I'm not some dumb kid. This time I'm fifty-one years old and I've got five billion dollars in the bank.

"I can hire enough lawyers to fight this thing for the rest of my life," I say.

"You may have to do that."

"You know what? You and Jim Bell want to rumble with me? Okay then, let's do it. You want war? I'll give you a war you'll never forget."

He says, "Steve. Please. Come on. It's not like that."

But he's lying and we both know it. Because it *is* like that. It's exactly like that.

"Think about the Dinsmore thing," he says. "At least consider it."

"Okay." I wait two seconds. "I just thought about it. The answer is no."

Once the Jim Bell story hits, everybody at Apple starts avoiding me like the guy with herpes at a hot tub party. I try arranging meetings, but everyone's busy. Their calendars are booked. Then I go down to the Apple gym for a workout and the guys who told me they were in Asia this week and couldn't meet are right there, hanging out with Jim Bell and yucking it up. When they see me they get all weird and quiet and drift away. Worse yet, I swear one day when I'm riding my Segway across the campus I catch a glimpse of Mike Dinsmore ducking into the iPhone building. Sure, I was far away, but it's pretty hard to miss a six-foot-five-inch giant with bright red hair. I did a quick U-turn and zipped over there and demanded to be let in. The Israelis refused. By the time I got security clearance and barged into the building, Goliath was long gone.

Even the shipping dock idiots seem to know I'm in trouble. One day I'm walking past one of the docks and from inside, in the shadows, some guy yells out, "Dead man walking!" and then a bunch of morons start laughing their nuts off.

So yeah. It's like that. Whatever. I can deal. It's September, my favorite time of the year, when we get the best weather in the Bay Area and everyone comes back from their summer vacations and business at Apple starts to buzz as we all gear up for the December quarter, which is usually our busiest time of the year. I spend my days with Ja'Red, meditating and working out on the climbing wall and drinking smoothies and getting stoned and brainstorming about where the computer industry is going. It's good to have at least one quasi-pal to hang around with, even if he is half my age and walks around dressing and acting exactly like me and is always bugging me about some new product idea, like the computer he's designed that's just a sheet of plastic that you can roll up and carry with you in a tube, with all the guts and circuitry wired into the plastic.

"That's total shit," I tell him. "Absolutely shit."

He tells me I'm wrong, that he's done some research with component suppliers and research labs in Japan, and right now the parts are too expensive but if you plot the expected price declines on a curve you can see the whole thing hitting a sweet spot where you can build one for less than two thousand dollars by the year 2012.

"The cost is not the point," I tell him. "Nobody wants a computer that's a piece of plastic rolled up in a tube."

"You can roll it out on the table in front of you, and type on the plastic. The keyboard will be in the screen."

"That's shit," I say. "It's a shit idea. Don't waste your time."
This makes him so upset that he starts crying. "I'm not going
to give up on this," he says.

Fair enough. I admire his passion. Plus the fact is that while
his idea may be insane it's no crazier than the stuff we used to
dream up back in the early eighties. Back in those days all of our
ideas were insane. Ja'Red, in fact, is lot like the guys who built
the original Macintosh. They were young, and had no real computer training, and in the end, as it turned out, they could not
actually produce a working computer. But they had vision, and a
huge sense of their own specialness, which is what really counts.

Right now we need a few wackos like Ja'Red at Apple. The
world of technology is a very confusing place. Nobody really
understands how things are going to play out. Do the cable guys
win? The TV networks? The Internet portals? The movie stu-
dios? The music labels? The media companies? Honestly, I have
no idea. I would never admit this to anyone, but Ja'Red has as
good a grasp of how things are going to shake out as I do.
He's smart. Really smart. Just uneducated, which, frankly, is an
advantage.

Look at the greats—me, Bill Gates, Larry Ellison, Picasso,
Hemingway, Leonardo, Michelangelo, Stephen Hawking. They're
all dropouts. The way I see it, for really smart people, education
only serves to clog your creativity and shut down your brain. I
like to imagine the brain as this giant honeycomb, and you start
off with all these millions of open cells, but every book you read,
every class you take, every piece of math you learn is a little plug
that gets stuck into a cell and seals it shut. If you happen to get
an MBA it's like going back and double-sealing the doors with
cement.

Which is why, in fact, I'm so glad that I have almost no education at all. And why I've started letting Ja'Red attend some of
our design and strategy meetings. He's supposed to be there to

listen and take notes, but of course he starts talking and trying to take over and convincing everyone of his genius. Nevertheless I keep inviting him, because it gives me great pleasure to see all these assholes who won't talk to me anymore get tormented by some kid. Ordinarily I do the annoying myself. But this is great. I've got a proxy. And he's good at it. One day he tells the retail guys they should replace all the clear glass in our Fifth Avenue store with black smoked glass, and use lasers to create holographic robot greeters who will stand in the doorway to all our stores and guide customers to the right section. They practically start foaming at the mouth.

The September quarter marks the end of our fiscal year, and it's a total blowout, our best year ever. Our computers are gaining market share, and the iPod remains the top music player, with no real challengers. We've got record sales, soaring profits, ten billion dollars in the bank. Our stock is on fire. A little quick math reveals my own net worth is up several hundred million dollars in the past month alone.

But of course nobody in the management suite is going to give me any credit for how well we're doing. They still won't talk to me or take my phone calls. Fair enough. You know what I do? The night of our earnings announcement, after everyone else has gone home, Ja'Red and I walk around the executive suite tacking up copies of the current earnings release next to the same release from ten years ago, in 1996, when the company was in the crapper. I use a real hammer and big huge nails, just like Martin Luther King—the original one, from the Dark Ages, not the Jr one from the 1960s.

"They're not going to push me out of here," I tell Ja'Red afterward, when we're cruising up the 101 to the city for a visit to Brandy Ho's in Chinatown. "Money talks and bullshit walks. They can't run this place without me, and they know it."

Overall things are quiet and peaceful, just the way they should be. Tom Bowditch is away in Asia assassinating government officials or hunting endangered species or doing whatever it is he does with his free time, so I'm spared his dog breath and spittle. Francis X. Doyle appears to be leaving us alone. Bobby DiMarco checks in every so often, but only to reassure me that there's nothing going on with the investigation. To be sure, Sampson and his gang are still toiling away in the Crosby conference room, digging through their "irregularities," but at least we've switched them over to Macs so I don't have to hear those moronic Windows rebooting honks every fifteen minutes. Down in engineering, the iPhone team is making some progress, though they're still struggling to come up with a circuit board that looks beautiful and works right.

Of course the mutineers are still up to their dirty tricks, and the anti-Steve propaganda campaign continues, but there's no real damage. *Wired* runs an article that purports to tell the inside story of how the iPod was first created, and gives all the credit to a bunch of guys that nobody has ever heard of, and the only mention of me is where they say that, ironically, when these geniuses first came to me with the iPod proposal I told them it was "total shit" and shot it down. Only through their courage and perseverance were they able to push the product through anyway, and then when the iPod became a hit, in rushed El Jobso to steal all the credit. This is the new official version of events.

Ja'Red says it's a total hatchet job and full of factual errors. Poor kid. He really thinks I invented the iPod. He says we should file a libel suit.

We're in my office getting high before lunch. I explain to him that, just as with the *Journal* story about Jim Bell, this *Wired* story didn't happen by itself.

"This was teed up by people inside Apple."

He's like, "Dude, no way."

I'm like, "Dude, way."

He points out that the story claims nobody at Apple would speak to *Wired*. I point out that in fact the story says nobody at Apple would speak *on the record*.

"It's a coup," I explain. "My own foot-soldiers have set themselves to the ignoble task of un-writing the Legend of El Jobso and smoothing the way for my successor."

"Whoa," he says. "For real? That's intense."

"Totally." I'm still marveling at the fact that I managed to get out a sentence like that, using words like *ignoble*, which is pretty amazing when you consider how baked we are.

"It's like a tragedy by Ibsen," I say. "Or is it Chekhov. I always get them confused."

He gives me this look and says, "Huh?"

This is a little embarrassing, but every year, on the day when they announce the Nobel Peace Prize winners, I clear my schedule and sit by the phone. I know it's silly. Larry says I'm an idiot. You know what? I wish I could be like him. Just vapid and self-centered and caring about nothing about racing giant penis boats and sleeping with Asian interns. But I can't. I want more from life. I want to make a difference. I care too much. That's my fatal flaw.

I tell myself, *Just don't even think about it.* But I can't help it. I get my hopes up. Then they announce the winner and I'm crushed. I mean, nothing against the guy this year, the Bangladeshi banker who micro-loaned money to Third World people or whatever. Very cool idea.

It's just that, well, I kind of feel that what I've done for the world has had a little more impact than some bank in Bangladesh. Maybe to some people a computer or a music player just seems like a piece of consumer electronics. But there's another way to look at these objects, and in this other way of looking at them, which is the way we look at them in Cupertino, well, let's just say you could kind of start to see these devices as being kind of transformative, in a cultural kind of way.

But no. They give the prize to the micro-loan guy.

What's more embarrassing is that this year I had Ja'Red put together a presentation to send to the Nobel people describing our products and also describing my plans for the Apple World Peace Summit, which is something I've been trying to arrange where we'll bring together all the bad guys from around the world and all the good guys too and then we'll all just talk, and we'll have featured hosts like Bill Clinton, Nelson Mandela, and Bono.

One of the marketing dicks got wind of this and pulled some attitude, pointing out that (a) you can't lobby for the Nobel prize; and (b) the peace summit hasn't even happened yet, and chances are it never will; and (c) shouldn't we be concentrating on how to manage this little options scandal?

Fair enough. The guy had a point, though it doesn't matter since he's no longer working here. We are going to pay his hospitalization and plastic surgery bills, though, because that's just how we do things at Apple.

By seven o'clock on the day of the awards I'm still hanging around in my office, still thinking maybe they're going to realize they made a mistake and they're going to call me or something. Finally Ja'Red sticks his head in and says, "Dude, it's like three in the morning over there in Sweden. You want to go get some pizza or something?"

We're heading out when the phone rings. I rush back, like a schoolgirl. But it's not the Nobel people. It's Bono. He asks me if I saw the Nobel stuff. I pretend I didn't. He tells me it was some banker, and then lets slip that he, Bono, was one of the finalists. "Fookin amazin, isn't it?" he says.

Of course I try to be all positive and happy for him, but inside I'm dying. My stomach is just in knots. I mean, come on. Bono makes the short list and I'm still out here pounding my pud?

"Steve," he says, "do me a favor and don't tell anyone about it, okay? I'd really rather not have people knowing about it and thinking I'm bragging about it, because God knows I'm not. I haven't told anyone except The Edge, and he didn't even know what the fookin prize was. He thought it was something from MTV. But yeah, it was me and Cindy Sheehan and Ahmadinejad up for the peace prize."

"Ahmadinejad? Is he the micro-loan dude?"

"Naw, man, he's the shah of Iran."

"I thought the shah of Iran died a long time ago."

"This is the new shah, the one they just elected last year. Me and Geldof had lunch with him. He's totally all about bringing peace to the region."

"So what's up with this micro-banker guy?"

"That's what I told the Swedes. I was like, 'How many times has this guy been to Africa? Has he fathered any children there? Because I have. Has he held hands and posed for photos with people who have AIDS? Because I have.'"

"What's the guy's name? I'd never even heard of him."

"Fook if I know, and man, I'll tell ya, who knew that all you had to do to win the Nobel Peace Prize was go around handing out ten-dollar bills to poor people, right? Can't do it now, though, cause it's been done. Gotta think of something else. Like maybe this AIDS thing where we do the red products. But I was thinking about that too and you know what? Keepin these Africans alive isn't gonna do nothing fer peace is it? I mean it just means there'll be more of the fookers who can chop each other to bits with machetes, innit? I dunno. Like you say, brother, Peace. Right? Pay it forward. Peace."

"Sure thing," I say. "Peace, my brother. Power to the people."

I'm not a superstitious person—well, okay, actually I am. And somehow this Nobel thing strikes me as a bad omen. It's like I can feel my karma taking a downward plunge. Sure enough, a few days later Bobby DiMarco calls and informs me that I'm going to be sitting down with U.S. Attorney Francis X. Doyle for a deposition.

"You got any asbestos underpants?" he says. "Ha! Kidding. Don't worry. I'll be there with you. I won't let anything bad happen to you, honey."

"Could I get you something? Water? Coffee? Juice? Something to eat? We've got bagels. And muffins."

This is Francis X. Doyle, working very hard to seem like the world's all-around most friendly and nonthreatening guy. He's wearing a navy blue suit that looks like he bought it at Sears, and I'm sure underneath his white shirt his little man-nipples are totally erect just thinking about how today is the most important day of his life and this deposition is going to send him soaring into the governor's office.

So I ask for water and he actually fetches a bottle of Dasani and brings it to me himself, which is a trick I've seen Jeffrey Katzenberg use and which on one level conveys that he's a super humble and down-to-earth guy, but at the same time also establishes up front that he's in control, because you asked him for water and if you want the water you have to reach up and take it from his hand, blah blah.

It's ten in the morning and we're in the San Francisco U.S. Attorney's office, a suite of rooms on the eleventh floor of a horrifically ugly office building on Golden Gate. The place has all the charm of a Soviet parking garage, and all I could think when we were walking in was, "Who creates buildings like this? Who sits down with the blueprints and says, Wow, yes, this is *fantastic*, we *must* build this?"

It's all very relaxed and comfortable, lots of dark wood, a brown leather sofa, two leather armchairs, nice lamps on the side tables, sort of old-boy Harvard Club shabby chic. Doyle talks about the weather, and his kids, and the traffic he hit coming in from Marin this morning. He tells me he's been using Macs since his undergraduate days at Dartmouth in the eighties. He loves the iPod too, and so does his son, who wants him to get my autograph, ha ha ha, isn't that something. He says he's really sorry to drag me up here, but it's his job to talk to everybody.

I know what he's trying to do. He's trying to get me to relax and let my guard down. I smile, and say as little as possible. I've been fasting and meditating for three days, and I'm totally Zen focused.

A door opens, and in walks William Poon carrying a Sony laptop and making a big deal of letting me see him slipping his Microsoft Zune music player into the pocket of his suit jacket.

Poon is short and slim and bristling with nervous energy, rocking up on the balls of his feet and rolling his shoulders like a boxer. His hair is wet, as if he's just come from lifting weights at the gym. He's eager and edgy and wound super tight, in the way that only Asian dudes can be.

Doyle seems weird around him, almost subservient, as if he were working for Poon rather than the other way around. Certainly it's weird that Poon came in after Doyle did; at Apple I'd never let that happen.

"I'd like to introduce Assistant U.S. Attorney William Poon," Doyle says.

We shake hands, and I can't resist. "I'm sorry, what's your name again?"

"William Poon." He tries to make it sound like "pone."

"Poon?"

"Don't start." He gives me a tight smile.

"Excuse me?"

"You can just call me William."

"What are you, touchy about your name or something?"

"Look, I've heard all the jokes already. How about we keep this professional."

"Sure thing, Poon. By the way, did you know Bobby D. and I were in Nam together?"

Bobby gives me this look, as if to say, *What the fuck is wrong with you? Are you fucking mental?*

Poon says, "That's very nice for you."

"I just thought you might be interested."

"Why, because I'm Asian? My parents are from Singapore."

"Same thing, right?"

He laughs, but I can tell he's getting pissed. "You must be pretty ignorant if you think Singapore is the same thing as Vietnam," he says.

I put up my hands and say, "Hey, back off, Bruce Lee."

"I don't believe this." Poon's face is getting red, and his left eye has begun to twitch.

Doyle puts his hand on Poon's arm and says, "William, it's okay. Calm down."

"That's right," I say. "Do what the white man tells you, Kato."

"Oh you did *not* just say that." Poon looks like he is working very hard to keep his head from exploding.

"Are you serious? That's just fucking racist."

"I think *you're* a racist," I say.

"That doesn't even make sense."

"You know," I say, "your hostility is upsetting me. And your bias is very evident. I think you should recuse yourself."

He starts sputtering. Doyle takes him off to another room to cool down.

While they're gone Bobby pulls me aside and tells me to cut the shit. "I'm serious," he says. "Don't fuck around with this guy."

"I'm just trying to rattle him."

"Well, don't, okay? Do us both a favor."

The deposition takes place in a room with a conference table, big leather chairs, a microphone on the table and a videocamera pointed at me. This is what we expected. I've been rehearsing in a studio that looks almost exactly like this. A court stenographer sits at the end of the table, along with three of Doyle's associates, two guys and a woman, who sit with folders and stacks of paper and again those heinous Windows laptops—in this case, Dells, which are the worst of all. I try not to look at them. But there is no avoiding the sound of their fans, whirring and droning.

The assistant lawyers introduce themselves. They can barely conceal the fact that they are psyched to be meeting me. But I also know what they're thinking: *Wow, I am so going to make a fortune in the private sector after I put this asshole in prison.*

"Nice to meet you too," I say to each of them. "A real pleasure."

On my side I've got Bobby D and fifteen lawyers from Apple who are each being paid four hundred bucks an hour to sit here and look formidable.

Doyle and Poon sit directly across from me. Doyle does the talking. Poon just sits there glaring at me and sliding questions to Doyle. They start out with easy questions, like my name, my date of birth, and my title at Apple. For each question, no matter what he asks, I pause for three minutes, with my hands pressed together. Then I ask Doyle to repeat the question. On questions that are more complicated than name, rank, and serial number, I look for tiny discrepancies between the way he asks the first time and the way he asks the second time, and then I ask him which question he'd like me to answer.

It's a strategy called "Zen Crazy," which I learned in the seventies when I was studying at the Los Altos Zen Center. The concept comes from Zen monasteries. Certain monks go bonkers from the isolation and turn into these super annoying assholes who go around bugging the shit out of the other monks. In Buddhism these guys are tolerated, and even revered, because it's believed that their craziness is actually a way of channeling the divine. And even though what they're saying may appear to be random or senseless, it often contains some higher truth.

Of course in the West if you do this you're considered a mental case, and they throw you out of your own company. Which is why at certain periods of my life I've come very close to chucking everything and disappearing into a monastery, where I could be a complete dick and get worshipped for it. But then I realized—that's pretty much the deal I have at Apple.

Eventually Francis X. Doyle starts getting exhausted.

"Would you like to take a break?" he says.

I tell him no, I'd rather push on. Through meditation I've managed to lower my pulse rate into the thirties, while Doyle is starting to sweat, and his aura has gone from a white-blue when we began to an orange-red. Poon's aura has been glowing like the center of the sun the whole time.

We take a break anyway, because Doyle apparently has some bladder control issues, and when we reconvene he starts trying to trick me, asking the same questions multiple times but from different angles and in slightly different ways, seeing if I'll trip up. I'm concentrating as hard as I can. No matter what he asks, I pause, wait, and ask for the question again. Then I pause again, and instead of answering, I'll say, "Yeah, I don't know." Or, "Yeah, I don't remember." Or, "Pass. Next category."

After six hours they let me go. Poon makes a big deal of letting me see him put on his Zune headphones. He won't shake my hand.

Outside I'm totally pumped. Bobby, however, looks suicidal.

"What do you think you were doing in there?"

"Are you kidding? I friggin *owned* that guy. We should go have a drink and celebrate."

"Some other time."

He walks off, looking grim. Whatever. I was there, and I know how it went: I nailed it. I'm so psyched that I race straight home and drink a tiny bowl of miso soup, the first thing I've eaten in three days, and then run upstairs to the Home Pod and take off all my clothes and stand in front of the mirrors going, "You talking me? You talking to *me?* Well then who are you talking to? 'Cause I'm the only one here."

Seriously, I am the coolest person I've ever met.

40

Next morning I arrive at work to find Tom Bowditch parked outside in his Maybach. I pull into my usual handicapped space and get out to see what he's doing here.

"Get in," he says. He's wearing his navy blue business suit, and he's not yelling and spitting. He just sits there saying nothing at all. The driver heads south on Route 85 and then up Route 17 into the Santa Cruz Mountains.

"I talked to Bobby D," Tom says. "He says you screwed the pooch pretty badly."

"What's that supposed to mean?"

"Literally it means you had sex with a dog. But I'm speaking figuratively. Apparently things didn't go well with Doyle."

"No way. They got nothing out of me."

"Bobby says you provoked them. You told that Poon kid that you cut off his mother's ears or something? Jesus. *Before* they were pissed. Now they want your head on a platter."

"What's Bobby DiMarco doing telling you about my interview? What about attorney-client privilege?"

"No such thing. Anyway, kid, here's the thing. Sampson and his guys have found some more problems."

"You know what? I want Sampson fired."

"Well I wanted to diddle Angie Dickinson, kid, but you know what? It didn't happen. Here's the thing. This isn't about you anymore. It's about the company. And the shareholders. It's about my investment. My money. You understand? Kid, I've made a lot of money thanks to you. I've got a five-x return on my investment in ten years. You've done right by me, and I appreciate that. Nevertheless, if it were up to me I'd be in favor of firing you right now, or having you killed and making it look like an accident. But luckily for you, we ran some computer modeling scenarios and found out that if you were fired, or killed in a plane crash, the stock takes a thirty percent hit, day one. I hope you take comfort in that."

"Sure," I say. "I'm feeling real comfortable right now."

I reach for the door handle. I figure we're going about forty miles per hour, and if I jump out and roll just right I could survive with a couple of broken bones or maybe a concussion. But Tom's a step ahead of me. He clicks the door locks shut. I grab the handle anyway.

"Don't bother," he says. "Now listen, Rain Man. Did you not hear what I just told you? You're not going to get hurt. We need you. We've got to protect you. As personally distasteful as this may be to me, it's what we have to do. So. This means we need to sacrifice some others. You familiar with the Aztecs?"

"Yeah, they built this huge system of highways in Peru, and it's totally amazing."

"That was the Incas. The Aztecs were in Mexico. They practiced human sacrifice. The idea was, to appease the gods, they would sacrifice some captives. Same thing now for us. We need to figure out who's going to get killed. I figure the first victim is Sonya Bourne. She's already lawyered up, and she walked out in the middle of all this, so what the hell. She's dead to us, right?"

"Sure," I say. "No problem."

Maybe this sounds cruel. I've known Sonya for twenty years. She worked with me at NeXT, and came to Apple with me when I returned. She's one of my oldest quasi-friend type people, and I happen to know that her husband has recently been diagnosed with some weird Stephen Hawking–type wasting-away type disease. In other words, she's a perfect candidate. Because if she's actually convicted of anything, her husband's illness will be something she can use at sentencing to get her some leniency.

"Okay, so we've got Sonya. But one scalp isn't gonna do it. Who else?"

"Jeez," I say, "I don't know. Jim Bell maybe?"

"Good one. Seriously."

We're driving along Skyline Boulevard, close to Neil Young's ranch, and I'm thinking maybe we should pull in and see if he's home. We could go in and talk politics for a while and smoke some weed and Neil can give me shit about how music sounds better on vinyl than on an iPod.

"Listen," Tom says. "How much do you like Zack? You're pretty close with him, right?"

"When I had cancer, he visited me every day in the hospital. And his wife brought food over to our house."

"So you're pretty close."

"Very close."

"So would you throw him under a bus? I mean, if you had to? To save your own ass?"

"Tough question. Let me think about that." I press my hands together and pretend to think. "Um, yes."

"Kid, you're amazing. You know that? You've got no loyalty at all, do you? I love it. I really do. It's why you're one of the great ones. You remind me of Lou Gerstner sometimes. And he was, in my opinion, the greatest of the great."

41

Poor Zack shows up for the board meeting and he has no idea that he's about to get sucker-punched. Everyone else has been prepped for the vote, and yes, fair enough, it's against the law for members of a board of directors to meet in secret without notifying all the members, but at this point we're so far around the bend that illegal meetings are the least of our worries.

We begin with a presentation by Charlie Sampson in which he summarizes the problems that his team has discovered so far. Tom thanks Sampson and says we need to deliberate in private. As soon as Sampson leaves, Tom says it is clear that Zack was deeply involved in this malfeasance and for the sake of the company he is presenting a motion that Zack should step down from the board.

Zack starts to protest, but he's stammering pretty badly, and before he can say anything, the board has voted. Zack starts blabbering about how if we're going to vote about him then we should be taking a vote of confidence in me, too, because if he was involved then certainly I was involved.

Tom ignores this and hands Zack a letter of resignation to sign. Bing! The light goes off in Zack's head and he realizes the meeting was a setup.

"I'll want to have my lawyer look this over before I sign anything," he says.

"Sure thing," Tom says. "Meanwhile, until you do sign it, for your own safety, we're going to have some security guys from Las Vegas watch your wife and kids for you."

Zack starts to cry. He knows it's over. He signs the paper and runs out of the room, slamming the door behind him.

Maybe this makes me an old softie, but I have to admit that for a few seconds I really feel bad for Zack. He's an incredibly nice guy. Really honest. A good soldier, as they used to say. On the other hand, as Tom points out, Zack won't do much prison time. Twelve to eighteen months at the most. And it's not like he's going to be in some super-max or anything.

But I quickly put the whole thing out of my mind because, as I've learned over the years, guilt is just this huge energy blocker. Mostly I'm just relieved that it's over.

I figure we're done. So I get up to head for the door. But Tom says, "Um, Steve? Hold on a sec."

I turn back. None of the board members will look at me.

"Sit down," Tom says.

Turns out Zack isn't the only one getting sucker-punched. Tom informs me that, effective today, the company is going to have research and development reporting to Jim Bell instead of to me. Same for engineering and design. Jim's already got manufacturing and sales, plus marketing and public relations, so what this means, basically, is that now the whole company reports to Jim.

"So I've been stripped of all day-to-day responsibility," I say.

"That's not it at all," Tom says.

"Really? Because unless I'm mistaken, I don't think we have any other divisions, dude."

"We're not taking anything away from you," Tom says. "We're freeing you up so you can be more creative. We're starting a new products group, and we're putting you in charge of it."

"To do what? The iPhone?"

"I thought we were using a code name for that. Geronimo or something."

"Guatama."

"Whatever."

"Right. So am I running that project?"

"Actually, no. That's being rolled into engineering."

"So what am I supposed to work on?"

"Whatever you want. That's the beauty of it. New stuff. Next-generation stuff. Oh, and one other thing. We've hired Mike Dinsmore back and put him over the, um, the phone thing. Guantanamo or whatever."

"You can't do that."

"We can, and we already did."

"I fired that freak for a reason," I say.

"A stupid reason. We hired him back for a better reason."

I look at the rest of the board. "You're all voting with Tom on this?"

They all kind of shrug and nod. None of them dares to actually speak to me—they're not that bold yet—but it's clear they're no longer in my camp.

"We're setting you up with a secret skunk works," Tom says. "An advanced research lab in Palo Alto. Close to your house."

"So now I can't even come in to work here at my office?"

"You can do whatever you want. But we thought you'd like your own lab, and this space became available in Palo Alto, so we took out a lease. We wanted to surprise you. We thought you'd be excited! Steve, we need to get you thinking again. We don't want you distracted by being dragged into all this crap with the SEC. We need you in an environment where you can create. Do anything you want with the building. Hire I. M. Pei or Frank Gehry. Go wild. Take a dozen of the best engineers, anyone you want. Go back to your roots, like when you invented the Macintosh. Be a pirate again. Think outside the box. We need you to invent the future of this company."

"If that's the case," I say, "why does it feel like you're throwing me out of an airplane at thirty thousand feet?"

"That," Tom says, "is something you need to take up with your therapist."

Mrs. Jobs is in Atherton attending a birthday party for some venture capitalist's five-year-old kid when I reach her. "Same old same old," she says. "Pony rides, jugglers, clowns. They've got Cirque du Soleil from Las Vegas, because Debbie hired them for Noah's party so now everybody has to do it. Then at three they've got Sammy Hagar doing a solo acoustic set."

"I thought they were getting Sting."

"Sting wanted a hundred thousand bucks, and Sammy does it for ten, and the kids don't know the difference, so who cares. What's up?"

"I think I just got thrown out of my company again."

"You what?"

I explain about the meeting.

"Can they do that?" she says.

"They just did."

"You should leave anyway. They don't deserve you. How about we do some traveling? You want to go to Nepal? We should go before all the snow melts from the global warming."

"I'll think about it."

"Poor baby."

"I know."

"It's the price you pay for the gift you have. Nobody ever loves an artist."

"Yeah."

"What's the matter?"

"I don't know." My eyes are starting to well up. I don't want her to hear me cry. "I should go."

"Oh shit, hold on," she says. There's commotion in the background. "Shit, some kid just fell off the climbing wall. I'll call you
back, okay? I love you."

"Love you too," I say, but she's already hung up.

Ross Ziehm puts out a press release announcing that we've
found yet more problems with our accounting. We include a
quote that Ross wrote for me in which I apologize to the shareholders and pretend to be contrite. We also announce that Sonya
has left the company and that Zack is leaving the board. We're
pretty sure people can read between the lines and understand
that those two are to blame for everything, and that I'm just the
victim of their shenanigans.

By evening the announcement has hit all the news sites and
all the investor shows on TV. As expected, they skewer Zack and
Sonya and gloss over any mention of me.

Next morning when the market opens our stock has gone *up*
two dollars. *On bad news.* This is the power of communications.
It's one area where Apple really outperforms every other company in the world, and I'm really proud of what we've managed
to achieve.

I'm home having breakfast when Zack calls. He's sobbing,
which is really annoying because I'm really trying to focus on my
cantaloupe. Also, he's back in his full-blown stammering and
stuttering mode, which I swear is worse for me than it is for him.

"Steve," he says, "h-h-h-how could you d-d-d-do this to
me?"

He says he never got anything out of this, and it was all for
my benefit, not his own, and he was doing it to help me, he bent
the rules because he was loyal to me, and because he was my
friend.

"And n-n-n-now," he says, "you're throwing m-m-m-me to
the w-w-w-wolves?"

"Zack, I think you're being a little bit melodramatic here, don't you?"

"To the *w-w-w-wolves,* Steve. You're throwing me to the *wolves.*"

I do my Zen thing and start talking to him in riddles. I tell him the story of the Zen master who was asked by a student, "If you believe in freedom, why do you keep your bird in a cage?" So the Zen master opened the cage and the bird flew away out the window. The Zen master then told his student, "Now you owe me a bird."

Zack starts screaming. "What the f-f-f-fuck are you t-t-t-talking about? Jesus, Steve, you know what? You are s-s-s-so full of shit, do you know that? You really are. Well l-l-l-listen. No way am I going to go to jail for you. You wait and see."

I wait a moment. Then I go, "I'm sorry. I was checking my email. What did you say?"

Click. Dial tone. I hang up too. Mrs. Jobs looks up from her copy of *Mother Jones* and says, "You know, this global warming business really has me terrified. Have you read about these ice floes breaking off? It's really scary. Was that Zack? Are we still on for Saturday?"

"Yeah," I say, "I think that's probably not going to happen."

"What, because of this stock thing? He's really upset about this?"

"People are getting crazy over this stuff. He's acting like it's all personal or something."

"Well, it's like they say, at times like these you find out who your friends are. I guess Zack had us all fooled."

"Very true," I say.

"I listened to the tape," Tom Bowditch says. He means the recording of my call with Zack. Yes, we record everything.

"I wouldn't worry."

"You're not the one facing prison time."

"I'm going to send some guys to talk to him. Meanwhile, can I give you some advice? Be nice to Zack. Go see him. Indicate to him, in certain ways, that you're going to take care of him. You understand?"

"You mean offer him money?"

"Kid," he says, "you don't miss a beat, do you."

Paul Doezen hates Tom Bowditch. They've been at each other ever since Paul joined the company. During Paul's first board meeting Tom gave him a pop quiz, just to embarrass him. The questions weren't important. Tom asked him basic stuff, like what was our current ratio and how many days of inventory were we carrying on the balance sheet. There was no point to this. It was just Tom's way of making Paul look stupid and humiliating him in front of the board. Tom's a former finance guy himself and he likes to show off how smart he is. Plus, he'd wanted us to hire one of his friends instead of Paul, but the board voted against him and went with Paul instead. So he's made a point, ever since, of trying to trip Paul up.

So I'm not surprised when Paul tells me that during the course of his investigation into the short-selling and the leaks he's found some strange connections to Tom.

"I'm not saying we can connect the dots," he says. "It's just coincidences at this point."

We're at an Olive Garden in Palo Alto. I'm having a salad. He's having some kind of all-you-can-eat deal that features three kinds of pasta, three kinds of sauce, plus meatballs and sausage. It's sickening to watch, but also fascinating in a weird way.

"For one thing, short interest has doubled again," Paul informs me. "Which is partly to be expected, since the stock has been going up so much. But still. I don't know. It's weird. As for the guys in the Caymans, we didn't get much. The registrar is just some local guy, some lawyer. He's a front. But we did manage to track down some of their trades. That's where it gets interesting."

"But you don't have any smoking gun on Tom," I say.

He shakes his head. "All we have is that the Caymans company has done business with another Cayman company called MNA. That company, MNA, is owned in part by Luktev, which is a Russian oil and gas company. One of Luktev's minority shareholders is a company called the Fernway Group. Fernway's president is Christopher Winchester. He used to be deputy chair of the NSA. He went to Yale with Tom Bowditch. And they were both in Skull and Bones."

"I feel like I'm in a Michael Moore movie."

"There's more. Winchester's company, Fernway, also has a partnership on some Saudi oil fields and Dubai real estate with the Carlyle Group. Carlyle recently bought a twenty-five-percent stake in the Cho-Shabi casino in Macau."

"Which is owned by Tom Bowditch."

"Bingo." He spears a meatball with his fork and pops the entire thing into his mouth.

"So you think Tom is the one who's shorting our stock?"

"Maybe."

"What point would there be in Tom's shorting our stock? He's our biggest shareholder."

"Right. And he can't clear out his position because it would start a run on the stock. So maybe he's holding his shares, but he doesn't want to get crushed in a downturn, so he's buying shorts too. He's hedging. Or maybe he isn't our biggest shareholder anymore. Maybe he's unloaded his position, but he's done it in such a way that the transactions can't be traced. In which case he could be going short and actually trying to engineer a collapse of the stock."

"Dude," I say, "that's friggin nuts, even for you. Honestly. I mean, look, I know you don't like Tom. I know you guys have had your issues or whatever."

"That's not what this is about."

"Okay. Fair enough. But I'll be frank with you. I don't buy it. Tom's a fucker, but I don't think he's that kind of fucker, if you know what I mean."

He shrugs. "All I do is provide information," he says. "You do with it what you want." He eyes a piece of garlic bread on my plate. "You going to eat that?"

"Knock yourself out."

43

"**Roshi, my soul is troubled.** There is something I must ask you, but I fear I will offend you. May I speak from my heart?"

"Of course, Sagwa."

Ja'Red and I are walking through the gardens at the Green Gulch Farm Zen Center, north of San Francisco. Here on the farm we talk in a deliberately stilted manner, like characters in a kung fu movie, and we use Zen names. Ja'Red calls me "Roshi," which means "teacher." I call him "Sagwa," which I've told him is a Tibetan word for "student," though actually it's the name of a Chinese cat on a PBS Kids cartoon show.

It's a beautiful day for doing spiritual work: sunny, warm, a blue sky streaked with thin clouds. Down below us the ocean rolls, heavy surf heaving against black rocks.

"Roshi," he says, "you are an enlightened being. And yet . . . " He pauses. "And yet you do things that seem, well, cruel. You yell at people, and insult them, and treat them with disrespect. But at the same time you say that you want to make the world a better place. You say you want to restore a sense of childlike wonder to people's lives. How do you reconcile these things?"

It's a good question, and I've been expecting him to ask it. I remind him that Lao Tzu teaches us in the *Tao Te Ching* that to achieve perfection one must be ruthless. "Was it cruel of Siddhartha to abandon his wife and children? Was Buddha cruel to instruct his followers to beg for alms? One might say so."

He gives me this look—he's not buying it. The thing about Ja'Red is that he may be a stoner, but he's not stupid.

"Sagwa," I say, "our goal at Apple is to try to achieve perfection. Consider the iPod, or our Unix-based operating system. These are objects that approach perfection, and they could not have been realized if we were not ruthless in our design process. I believe that if Buddha were alive today he would recognize the wonder of our eighty-gigabyte video iPod. Does this help you?"

"Not really."

"You will need further contemplation. Devote this day to this one thought, that enlightenment requires cruelty."

We return to the temple in silence. I sense that I'm losing him.

The truth is, I've seen this coming ever since Ja'Red started hanging out in the cafeteria and talking to freakboy Mike Dinsmore and his pack of iPhone engineers. They're like a little band of mutineers, hanging out and talking shit about their Dear Leader. Now that Dinsmore managed to get himself re-hired the word has gone out across Apple that the iPhone engineering group is untouchable. They can do whatever they want, and they can't get canned. That's the message we've sent. Real smart, right?

Naturally Ja'Red tells me everything he hears from these guys, and he's always peppering me with questions. Did I really fire a guy for taking a day off to attend his mother's funeral? Did I really scream and cry and fire people because our delivery vans were not the exact same shade of white as our distribution building? Did I really refuse to give Apple stock to a bunch of the earliest employees?

I find myself saying, "Yes, but . . ." a lot. As in "Yes, but the guy didn't have any personal days left, and it was his own fault, and he wasn't even that close with his mother." Or, "Yes, but people need to know that details are important and if the trucks don't match the buildings, I can't concentrate." Or, "Yes, but I was the one who came up with all the ideas, and I'm the one who had to rob convenience stores to get money to make payroll in the early days, and I'm the one who took all the risk, so why should all these other guys get to come along for a free ride when it was time to cash in?"

My fears about Ja'Red are confirmed on the ride home in the limousine when he starts hitting me with more questions, like "Isn't it weird to go to a Buddhist retreat in a limo?" and "Didn't Buddha, like, give up his kingdom to seek enlightenment? So why don't you do the same?"

"Sagwa," I say, "I have no interest in money. My wealth could go away tomorrow and I wouldn't care. I didn't seek it out. I didn't ask for it. If anything, the money is a burden."

"Dude," he says, "I read the papers, okay? You forced the company to pay you more money than they wanted to pay you. They offered you one thing, and you demanded more. You have five billion dollars, you're one of the richest people in the world, and yet you still haggled with them for like eight months over how much they were going to pay you."

He suggests that I should give away all of my money. This is something every rich person hears eventually and honestly it is just about the stupidest suggestion in the world. Think about it. What point would there be in making money if you were just going to give it away? But I don't say that. Instead, I take a deep breath, and fold my hands in front of me, and I do the thing where I act like I'm taking his comments very, very seriously, even though really I'm thinking about something completely different, like what I'm going to have for dinner or something.

At last I speak, but when I do it's in this very soft voice, as if he's hurt my feelings but I'm going to forgive him for that and try to explain some higher truth to him.

"So here's the thing," I say. "I understand where you're coming from, because for a long time I struggled with the issue of money myself. I really did. And then, after a lot of contemplation, I had this really huge realization, which is this: *I'm not a regular person.* And there's no sense in me pretending to be a regular person. Jesus didn't go around being humble about who he was, did he?"

"Um, well . . ."

"Did Jesus pretend that he wasn't Jesus? No. He said, 'Dudes, I'm Jesus, and I'm the son of God, and you will all just have to deal with it, because I have to deal with this too.' It's the same for me. Do you think I enjoy this money? It's a curse. It's a cross for me to bear. I hope this doesn't sound vain. I'm not comparing myself to Jesus."

"Actually," he says, "I think you did."

"No," I say, "it was a metaphor. Now you suggest I should give away my money. Let's look at what happens if I do that. The poor people get the money and they rush out and buy fifty-inch flat-panel TVs and bags of crack and all sorts of other useless shit. No matter how much you give them, in two weeks they're back where they started. The money will flow through them and arrive back where it started, piled up with people like me. Does this make sense?"

"Not really," he says.

"Poor people are like sieves. Money just flows right through them. That's why they're poor. But for some special people, and like it or not I am one of these people, money gets drawn to us and attaches itself to us. There's like this aggregating force at work, a magnetic force. Money likes to be with other money. Money has an instinct. It seeks out certain people and sticks to them."

He says he still thinks there's a contradiction between the image I portray to the public of being all holy and pious and the reality of who I really am. I mean he's about *this close* to saying I'm a hypocrite.

I take one last run at him.

"Ja'Red, the only thing that any of us can do is to be who we really are. If you're Picasso, you paint. If you're John Lennon, you write songs. If you're Homer, you tell stories. You put your work out into the world and hope it helps people. If money comes to you, there is no way you can stop it. For me, right now, all I want to do is finish this iPhone and put it out into the world. Does that make sense?"

He doesn't answer. He just sits there, gazing out the window, looking either pissed off or depressed or both. When we drop him off at his house he gets out without saying good-bye. The next morning when I arrive at the Jobs Pod and greet him with a bow and say, "Namaste," he gives me this smirk and rolls his eyes and says, "Yeah right. Hey. Here's your green tea. Your mail is on your desk."

44

So fair enough, Ja'Red is disillusioned. It happens to everyone who gets close to me. First they worship me; then they realize I'm an asshole. But it's all a necessary part of the journey. Frankly I think failure and disillusionment are essential to personal growth. It happened to me when I was nineteen. I ran off to India and made a fool of myself. I went there hoping to study with a guru named Krishna Neeb Baba. He was an American, a psychology professor at Harvard who renounced his possessions and moved to India and supposedly had achieved enlightenment.

For a month I traveled along the Ganges, begging each day for my food and shelter. Krishna Neeb Baba's ashram was in the north of the country, in a pass surrounded by craggy mountains whose tips were covered in snow even in summer. Every day a stream of pilgrims trickled up the mountainside and gathered to hear the baba speak. Some stayed only a day or two. Others stayed for months. We ate one meal a day, and slept on a stone floor.

The baba was enormously fat, with a big mane of gray hair and a long flowing gray beard. He dressed in beautiful robes. Every day he would come sit with us and tell stories. Then he would leave. That was it. Sometimes he would not speak at all, but would just sit in a trance and meditate, or lie down on a bench and sleep.

It took me ten days to realize that he was completely full of shit.

Apparently I didn't hide this very well because that day at the end of his sermon the baba singled me out and asked me to come with him on a walk. He asked me my name and where I was from. I told him. We stopped at a well. He washed my hair, then produced a razor and shaved my head.

"Do you know why I did this?" he asked.

"I think so." I was shaking, a little bit. This, in fact, was the reason I'd come all the way to India. It's what I'd always suspected about myself and wanted someone else to confirm. It's embarrassing to admit this, but even now, after realizing the guy was a fraud, there was still part of me that wanted him to tell me I was special.

"I'm the chosen one, right? I've always known it. I'm the reincarnation of Buddha, right?"

"Not quite." He scowled. "You have lice. That's why I shaved your head. You can't go home to America with lice."

"I'm going back to America?"

"Hey, you pick things up fast. Come on."

He led the way up a rocky path to a large stone house on the back side of the mountain. The house was huge, with wooden porches and a wood-shingled roof. Inside there were high ceilings, dark wood, enormous beams. The place was a palace, basically. The walls and floors were covered with Himalayan rugs. The baba had a pack of women waiting on him, including some very young teenage girls. There also were a lot of little kids running around and calling him "daadaa." I didn't ask.

Instead of the porridge and weak tea on which the pilgrims subsisted, the baba ate mutton and chicken, with lentil soup and side dishes of flavored rice and an eggplant dish that we ate with our hands, using pieces of hot bread. We sat on pillows at a low wooden table and ate until we were stuffed. The girls poured us tea and brought us clean plates for each new course of the meal.

"So you figured me out," he said. "Right? I could tell by looking at you."

"You mean that you're a fake?"

"Exactly. These sermons I give? I just make them up as I go along. I just say anything that comes into my head. They're pointless. You're smart enough to know that. That's why you're going home. There's no reason for you to stay here now that you know the truth."

"Our guru in Oregon told us you were a divine being. He came here four years ago and studied with you."

"From Oregon? Who's that? You mean Dave?"

"Baba Shripakdeva."

"Dave McMillan. I remember him." He reached into his mouth and pulled out a piece of gristly mutton and threw it on the floor. A girl ran over, picked it up, and hurried away. "What did he say?"

"He said you were divine. That you had achieved enlightenment."

"Shit. He knows better than to be spouting that guff. Young man, there is no divine. God is dead. Have you read Nietzsche? Have you heard of him at least?"

"I've read Nietzsche," I said.

"Well then what the fuck are you doing here?"

My face felt hot. I felt ashamed of myself—even though, let's face it, he's the one who should have been ashamed. Only he wasn't. He was completely happy with himself.

Outside, in the courtyard, kids were chasing each other, screeching. Through the open window we had a view of the mountains.

"So it's all a racket," I said. "You and Dave and all the rest of them, you're all in on it."

"Not at all. My goodness, no. It is not a racket. Most emphatically, no. Look, is Catholicism a racket? Is Christianity a racket? Or Judaism, or Islam? Just because you and I don't believe in those religions doesn't mean they're rackets. They serve a purpose. A very good and noble purpose. So do I."

"What, swindling people?"

"Helping people."

"Please."

"People need to believe in something. I become that something for them."

"You take their money."

"They give only what they want to give."

"They won't give much after I go back down there and tell them the truth."

"Yeah, see, that's the beauty of it. They won't believe you. Quite the opposite. They'll probably declare you a heretic, and stone you to death. That's the great thing about religious belief. We did studies on this back at Harvard. The power of faith, the ability of the human mind to believe in irrational things, the hunger for meaning, the need for God to exist—these are amazing things. That's the lesson for you. That's why I brought you here. That's the lesson you should take back with you to America."

"News flash: Con men are able to fool people. That's not exactly big news."

"The lesson," he said, shaking his head, "is that people are hungry for meaning, and they will go to great lengths to find it. Look at how far you came. Look what you put yourself through. Look at everyone around you in America. It's the wealthiest country that has ever existed in the history of the planet. Yet it's also the most miserable. Nobody is happy. How does that make sense? People have big cars, big houses, plenty to eat. Nothing works. They go to church. They go to shrinks. They drink, they take drugs. Or, like you, they give away all their possessions and fly to India. Only there's no answer here, either. As you are discovering today."

"I feel like an idiot."

"That's good." He smiled. "That's the first step toward learning something. Now let me leave you with a thought. America is all about commerce. That's what America is good at. Someone is going to figure out a way to create material things and to imbue them with a sense of religious significance. I don't know how this will happen. But it *will* happen, because it *needs* to happen." He held up his hands. "God on the one hand," he said, "and products on the other." He brought his hands together, and interlaced his fingers. "Whoever weaves these together will become more powerful than you can imagine." He stood up. "So," he said, "that's my lesson. Have a safe trip home to California. I'm going to take a nap."

One thing I love about the Valley is the way we combine our hyper-competitive work-hard-play-harder lifestyle with a desire to be socially responsible. Yes, people here have a lot of money. But almost everyone I know is also involved in philanthropy. So even while we're bashing each other's brains out in a sailing race or bike race or running race, we're also raising money to fight breast cancer or clean up the environment.

One of the best things we do is the annual party at Nigel Dryden's mansion in Woodside. Nigel is a Brit, but he's not uptight, I guess because he's been living here for so long. He originally came here as a tech reporter for the BBC. Then he became a venture capitalist, and got lucky—he was one of the early venture investors in eBay. These days he runs a blog about startups, and his blessing is considered a make-or-break thing for startups. Thumbs-up from Nigel means you'll get your Series A funding.

The Dryden (which is what everyone calls his party) happens every year in the fall, and the purpose is to raise money for the homeless. It's invitation only, to keep out the kind of strivers and start-up dorks who would use it as a chance to schmooze with A-listers like me and Larry Ellison. You pay five thousand dollars to attend, and there's a charity auction. The kicker is that everyone dresses up in rags and tattered clothing, so that we can see what it's like to be poor. Nigel got the idea from Bob Geldof, who has a similar party every summer at his castle in Ireland.

I know it sounds weird, but it's really effective, and everyone important shows up, from celebrity CEOs like Larry and me to the top venture capitalists and investment bankers. There's no press allowed, because unlike Hollywood, where no good deed occurs without camera crews present to broadcast the whole thing on some entertainment TV show, here in the Valley we don't like to be showy about our giving.

Only one party in the Valley draws a larger crowd than the Dryden and that's Mitchell Kaplan's Global Warming Beach Bash. People fly in from all over the world for that one. But the Dryden is far and away my favorite party, mostly because of the costumes. People get really creative. They spend huge amounts of money hiring designers and makeup artists. They show up with shopping carts filled with cans and bottles, or bring dirty sleeping bags and ripped-up blankets. Some bring little mangy dogs and cats, and hand-lettered cardboard signs saying things like WILL WORK FOR FOOD, or HOMELESS VET CLEAN AND SOBER NEEDS A BREAK.

This year's party is the biggest one ever, but it's a bit of a somber affair since some of the people here have been hit with criminal charges and the rest of us have an axe hanging over our heads. Talk about irony. Here we are, five hundred of the richest, most successful people in the Valley, doing yet another great thing for the world, making a huge difference in the lives of people less fortunate than ourselves, and we can't even enjoy it because some government hacks have decided to start hunting us for sport. Sure, we're all trying to smile and laugh as we're huddling around garbage cans with fires in them, but the whole thing just feels forced.

"Sorry to hear about your problems," Nigel says, sliding up. "Right-wing fascists, eh? But I'm glad you came. Good to get out and show your face."

"Oh, it's no big deal. We've looked into it. There's nothing."

This has become my standard response when anyone mentions the SEC investigation.

"Oh, I'm sure. Ridiculous. Crazy. Your tax dollars at work, right? Say, did you hear what we're doing later? After the auction? We're doing this Burning Man thing out on the back lawn. We've got two twenty-foot wooden statues around the back of the house. Paul Sarbanes and Mike Oxley. Sort of symbolic. Larry's idea. Brilliant one, I must say."

Larry takes a small bow. "Just my little way of making a statement," he says.

Larry's just had a combination face lift and eye job. He looks like he's been in a car accident—a really bad car accident. He also looks Japanese. Each time he goes in he has them make his eyes a little more slanted.

Waiters and waitresses in black formal attire are circulating through the crowd, delivering drinks and appetizers. The cool thing is that these people—the wait staff, the valets, the busboys and bartenders—are actual homeless people rounded up from shelters in the area.

"For a lot of these folks it's a chance to make a fresh start," Nigel says. "And they pick up a few bucks, which doesn't hurt."

"You don't let them in the house, do you?" Larry says.

"Please," Nigel says. "I'm generous, but I'm not crazy. Though I'll tell you, no matter how good the security is, we're always missing a few cases of booze by the end of the night. They're crafty, these folks, I'll give them that."

We're standing by a garbage can eating vegetarian egg rolls. Nigel is sporting old-fashioned hobo attire, with charcoal on his face and a kerchief tied to a stick. Larry's wearing baggy sweatpants, an old Army jacket, and mismatched shoes held together with duct tape. Mrs. Jobs and I are wearing layers of colorful pants and sweaters which my driver, Miguel, and his wife, Maria-Teresa, picked up for us in a Goodwill store up in East Palo Alto.

Suddenly a siren starts blaring and a dozen cops (actually actors in costume) swarm into the yard, shouting and waving nightsticks and shining flashlights in our eyes, pretending to be carrying out a "raid" on the "hobo camp." Not exactly a great idea, considering the way things are going in the Valley lately. Several dudes actually start running for the back hedges, until Nigel informs us that it's all stunt, and they're just here to herd us into the house for the auction.

We're almost at the door when I spot Tom Bowditch and Bobby DiMarco heading toward me from around the side of the house. They're not wearing costumes, and they're not smiling. I take this to be a bad sign. I'm correct.

"We need to talk," Tom says.

"My God, can't it wait?" Mrs. Jobs says.

They don't even bother to answer. Larry escorts Mrs. Jobs into the party. I follow Tom and Bobby around the house to Tom's Maybach.

"Doyle called me today," Bobby says, once we've settled ourselves inside the car. "Zack rolled. They flipped him. He's turning state's evidence."

"English, please," I say.

"Zack Johnson," Bobby explains, "has agreed to testify against you in exchange for a lighter sentence. Or possibly no sentence."

Tom leans forward in his seat. "They played Sonya and Zack off each other. Told them one of them was going to go free and the other was going to go to jail, and it was up to them to decide, but whoever rolls first gets the deal. Oldest trick in the book. Good one, too. It works."

"My bet," Bobby says, "is that they went to Sonya first, and she figured their first offer was shit and she'd wait for something better. So she turned it down, figuring Zack would know enough to do the same and then they'd come back to her with something better. Only Zack didn't pass. But who knows. It's entirely speculative."

"Point is," Tom says, "Doyle says he's ready to move on you. He was threatening to come here tonight and pick you up in front of the crowd. Wanted to make a splash."

"I backed him off for now," Bobby says. "But we're not going to be able to keep him off you forever."

We sit there for a minute. I'm not sure what to say. Bobby and Tom exchange a look, and then Bobby says he's going to step out of the car for a minute and stretch his legs.

"I want to give you some advice," Tom says, when we're alone. He opens the bar and pours us each a glass of Glenlivet. "This stuff I'm going to tell you, I'm going to say it once, and then once I've said it, I never said it. Okay? If I'm ever asked about this I'll deny I ever talked to you. Do you understand?"

I nod.

"I think you need to consider some drastic measures," he says.

"Finally! Yes! Thank God. I've been waiting for someone to say that. Who can we get to do it?"

"Do what?"

"Kill Zack."

"We're not going to kill Zack."

"Who are we going to kill then? Sonya?"

"We're not going to kill anyone."

"Why not?"

"Well, for one thing, it's against the law."

"I'm not saying we admit to doing it."

"We're not doing it, period."

"But it's a good idea. It's the most obvious solution. I mean, okay, it sucks for Zack. But for everyone else I think it's the best solution. Not just for me. But for the shareholders, the board of directors, the customers. Everyone."

"Steve, we're not going to kill anyone."

"But you said 'drastic measures.'"

"Look," he says. "Be quiet for a minute. Okay? Don't talk. Just listen." He takes a big drink of his Glenlivet, then pauses and takes another gulp, draining his glass. "There's this program," he says. "Sort of like the witness protection program. You can get out of the country. You can get a new identity, change your appearance. There are people I know who can help you do this. I'm telling you this as your friend."

"I'd rather just kill Zack. Seriously. You sure we can't do that?"

"I know it's a lot to digest," he says. "Think about it. Just don't think too long." He hands me a piece of paper with a name and phone number on it. "That's someone you should see. He's a plastic surgeon in Scottsdale. He's the one that did Princess Diana."

"But she's . . ."

"No. Not dead." He shakes his head. "Living with Dodi Al-Fayed in Qatar. This guy did Ken Lay too. Same thing. He's in

192

the South Pacific someplace, banging Polynesian girls. Living the good life. The heart attack was staged."

"No way."

"Why do you think they cremated the body? You remember who went to his funeral? Bush Forty-One and James Baker."

"You're messing with my head."

"It'll cost you a fortune. But it will keep you from going to jail. And if everything blows over, who knows? Maybe you can come back."

"I thought you told me the company was going to protect me. You said you had no choice. They couldn't survive without me."

"I did say that. It's true. They can't survive without you. But I don't see any way around it. Either you go to jail, or you fake your death and flee the country. Either way the stock gets killed. In which case you might as well save your own ass, don't you think? Right now my biggest concern is taking care of you."

"I still can't believe we're having this conversation."

"We're not," he says. "Remember? By the way, this guy in Scottsdale also did Sam Palmisano from IBM."

"Sam's not dead. He visited Apple six months ago. He thought the iMacs were flat-panel TVs."

"That didn't tip you off?"

"I figured, Hey, he's from IBM. What does he know about computers?"

"The real Sam died a year ago. Heart attack, at home, in bed. They didn't have a successor. So they created a Fake Sam. Gives them time to do a search for the next CEO. Soon as they find someone, Fake Sam gets the boot."

He opens the car door. Nearby, on the front lawn, Bobby D. is talking to an incredibly attractive bag lady who I would guess is some kind of PR flack. Something about the vacant look in her eyes, the fake smile. They all look like this. I think they go to a school someplace to learn how to do that smile.

Tom whistles. Bobby looks over and holds up one finger, as if to say, Just a minute.

"Guy never stops chasing pussy," Tom says. "It's his one weakness." He glances at my layers of pants and sweaters. "Nice outfit, by the way. First step toward your new identity. I like it."

Back inside the party, Mrs. Jobs is looking worried.

"It's nothing," I tell her. "No big deal."

She just looks at me. We've been married way too long for me to get away with whoppers like that.

PART THREE

Enlightenment

46

"**I'm not going to move,**" Mrs. Jobs says. "I'm not going to change my identity and have plastic surgery and get a new passport and go live in hiding. I'm sorry. I'm just not."

We're sitting in the kitchen, eating kiwi fruit for breakfast. I've been eating nothing but kiwi fruit for seven days and I feel amazing.

"We could go to Bali," I say.

"I've been to Bali. There's bugs."

"There's bugs everywhere."

"Well I don't need to live in Bali. I can go back to Bali anytime I want. I can go anywhere I want to go. But I'm not going to move. I love the Bay Area. It's the most beautiful, perfect, holistic, organic, self-righteous place on the entire planet. And the weather is sooo amazing. No. I won't move."

"We could live on a boat. We could travel the world."

"Why don't *you* go live on a boat. Go live on the moon."

Fair enough. She's angry. She says I must be guilty because if I were innocent I would stay and fight the charges and clear my name. I've told her it's not like that. The reality, I've told her, is that our government has been hijacked by fascists, and they've decided to target entrepreneurs and wealthy people.

"It's the same thing the Russians did in Czechoslovakia," I tell her.

"Honey," she says, "what you don't know about Czechoslovakia could fill volumes. Anyway, I talked to Nancy Johnson.

Zack told her what you guys did. You cooked the books."

"We did not cook the books. That is an absolute lie."

"Well that's what Nancy says."

"And you believe her? Did Nancy also tell you that she eats meat? Did she tell you that? It's true. She sends away on the Internet for those Omaha steaks. She cooks them when she's alone, when there's no one around. Zack caught her doing it."

"Look," Mrs. Jobs says, "I'm not moving to Bali. I'm not going to live on a boat like some fugitive. If you want to go, go."

Obviously things are not going well. Nevertheless I agree to meet with the CIA guy that Tom Bowditch recommended. We do this at the Garden Court, in the penthouse, which the guy has reserved under the name "Reinhardt."

We set the meeting for midnight, and I park down the street, hoping to avoid being seen. I enter through a side door, wearing a bulky coat and a baseball cap—and I'm spotted right away, as soon as I walk into the lobby.

"Good evening, Mr. Jobs!" beams one of the well-scrubbed kids whose job, it seems, is simply to hang around in the lobby and find ways to be annoying. This one, whose badge declares that his name is BRAD, and that he hails from SAN FRANCISCO, CA, holds the elevator door open for me and even offers to push the buttons for me. I assure him I can do this myself.

The elevator opens into a small foyer, opposite a door. I ring the bell. My host is about sixty, lean and tall, with gray hair cut short and the kind of anonymous, generically handsome face you see on Lands' End catalog models. Khakis, button down shirt, navy blazer. East Coast accent. Extremely formal. Offers me a drink. I take a bottle of water. He's having Scotch.

He introduces himself as Matt. Matt the part-time spy and part-time male model, I think. I assume that Matt is not this guy's real name. He doesn't mention credentials, and to be sure, Tom hasn't said explicitly that this guy is with the CIA, but I figure that must be where he's from. There's no small talk, no chit-chat, no discussion of my circumstances. The television is turned on and tuned to a Lakers game, with the volume turned up high—a precaution, I suppose.

"It's good we're talking now," he says, as we sit down across from each other in leather chairs. "Because as you can probably imagine, the sort of arrangement you're looking for can take a bit of time to set up. It's also expensive."

"How much?"

"If you have to ask, don't bother. This is last resort kind of stuff."

"Just give me a number."

"Five hundred million at the low end. Triple that is more likely in your case. More depending on how many family members are involved. Before you complain, remember what you're asking for. Remember what happens to anyone who gets caught helping you."

I suggest to him that it really would be much easier and much less expensive simply to have certain key people, for example Zack Johnson, terminated.

"Terminated?" He acts as if he doesn't understand.

"Terminated," I say, "with extreme prejudice."

He sits for a moment. "We don't do stuff like that," he says, and gives me this look that lets me know I'm lower than whale shit for even mentioning it. "Anyway, from what I understand about your situation, terminating people isn't going to solve your problem. There are records. Paper documents. Material on hard drives and tape backup systems."

I suggest that we could start a fire. We could burn down the Apple campus. "We've got insurance."

He tells me he's sorry but this is not the conversation he came here to have. The conversation he is here to have involves the ins and outs of how I disappear without leaving a trace. Easiest thing

199

is to go on vacation and stage my own death. Heart attack works best. Accidental drowning isn't bad either, he says. Taking the family is an option, but it will cost me.

He goes on for a while, like a travel agent pitching destinations and package deals, explaining things about passports and paperwork, transportation and housing, front companies and private jets.

"So," he says, wrapping up, "lots to think about, right?"

"You might say that."

"You know how to reach me," he says, and shows me to the door.

The whole meeting takes less than half an hour.

"What'd I tell you?" Larry says. "It's a government shakedown, plain and simple. Either they make you pay a fine, or they charge you up the ass to get you out of the country. Either way, the fuckers in the government get paid. Bottom line is, you've got money, and the government wants it."

Strictly speaking I'm not supposed to tell anyone about the meeting with Matt. But I need to talk to someone and Larry is the closest thing I've got to a friend. It's two in the morning and I'm at his Zen palace. I knew he'd be awake. Larry's like a vampire. He stays up all night and goes to bed at dawn. He sleeps in an oxygen-enriched room, which he claims gives him as much rest in four hours as a normal person gets in eight.

We're sitting in his home theater. When I arrived he was watching 9½ Weeks with his girlfriend. Now he's sent her away but the movie is still playing, with the sound off. Kim Basinger is crawling around on her hands and knees.

Larry says he's surprised that they won't even consider killing Zack. He offers to make a few calls for me on this. I shake my head. He passes me the bong. He's smoking this incredible red bud dipped in hash oil.

"Look," he says, "before you go all weird and radical and start thinking about disappearing off the face of the earth, have you at least considered meeting with Doyle?"

"I'm having urinal cakes made up with Doyle's face on them. Did I tell you that? I found a place in San Leandro that makes them."

"Go talk to him. See what he'll settle for."

"The guy wants my head on a plate."

"Correction. The guy wants to be governor. So give him what he wants. Let him win. Let him be the big hero who brought Steve Jobs to justice. Admit you're a bad guy, take your punishment, pay your fine. Do some community service, pretend to be sorry. What do you care? If you're smart you can turn it into a publicity stunt and end up coming out of it better than you went in. Plead guilty, pay a fine, go back to running your company. Fuckface can go run for governor and get his ass kicked by Arnold. I guarantee you the whole thing will cost a lot less than a billion dollars. I mean, what's at stake here? How much are they saying you made on these options? Twenty million bucks? So pay triple damages, sixty million, and throw in forty more as a tip for Attorney Shithead, and you're talking a hundred million. You can find that in the cushions of your couch."

"Uh huh." I'm kind of distracted by the weed. Or maybe by watching Kim Basinger with no clothes on. I'd forgotten how hot Kim Basinger used to be. I'm trying to remember if I dated her. I think I might have.

"One thing I do know," Larry says, "is that no way could you go live on an island and not do any work. You'd go nuts. Hey." He snaps his fingers in front of my face. "You there? Can you hear me?"

It takes me a long time to formulate a response.

"Dude," I say, "this stuff is amazing."

47

This time when we visit the U.S. Attorney's office we go straight to the conference room. This time it's just Doyle and Poon versus Bobby and me. No assistants.

"So you wanted to talk," Doyle says.

"No bagels this time?" I say. "No small talk?"

He gives me a tight smile. Bobby DiMarco has told me in advance to let him do all the talking, especially because last time I managed to antagonize Doyle and Poon so much that they almost refused to take this meeting. But then Bobby starts talking and he's just blabbering on, going mwah mwah mwah about about certain inducements and opportunities and risk assessments and benefits versus costs, and then Doyle starts doing the same thing back, and it must be some kind of lawyer-speak because they both really seem to be getting off on it.

Finally I just can't take it anymore and I go, "Look, can we please just speak English? This is very simple. All I want to do is work. It's the only thing that makes me happy. I don't care about money. This problem that I'm having with you idiots is a distraction. I just want to make it go away. I don't want to have to see you again. Okay? Nothing personal. But I'm busy. All I want to know is how much it will cost to make that happen."

Doyle says it's really not as simple as just walking in here and buying my way out of trouble.

"It's not like paying a traffic ticket," Poon says.

"Sure it is, Poontang. And here's an offer. Whatever profits you frigtards think I made that were inappropriate, I'll give them back. Plus I'll pay a fine of one hundred million dollars. I'll admit wrongdoing. I'll do community service."

"Wait, wait!" Bobby's in a panic. He turns to Doyle. "We're off the record, right? That's not an official offer."

"It *is* official," I say. "I'm sick of this shit."

Doyle sits there smiling. I guess he's amused to see DiMarco unable to control his client.

"So?" I say.

Doyle says he appreciates my candor, and he's glad that I've admitted to doing something wrong, but as he said before, this isn't a problem that I can make go away by paying a fine.

"We've been talking with Zack Johnson," Poon says. "We believe there may be more to this case than we realized. We're convening a grand jury."

I ask them how much money they think I could have made that I shouldn't have made. They both say they have no idea.

"If you have no idea," I say, "then what are you hassling me for? It's like arresting me for stealing a car, but saying you don't know which car I stole. Like, you'll figure that out later, after you've got me convicted."

"We're not going to get pushed into settling on a number," Poon says.

"Well, let me help you. My team figures it's about twenty million," I say. "I've offered to pay a fine that's five times that amount."

"And as we told you," Doyle says, "it's not that simple."

"So how about this. How about I pay a fine of one billion dollars?"

Bobby gasps.

"You can't just buy your way out of trouble," Doyle says.

"He's right," Bobby says. "And there's no way you're giving away a billion dollars."

I don't even look at Bobby. I'm staring at Doyle.

"A billion dollars. The offer is on the table. Biggest settlement ever made by any government agency. I'll do it right now. We shake hands and we bury this thing."

Doyle takes a deep breath, and shifts in his chair. He looks at Bobby.

"I don't think your client fully comprehends what's going on here." Then, to me, he says, "You can't just come in here throwing out some big number."

"I'm not just throwing it out. It's a real offer. And it's on the table." I slide an imaginary box onto the center of the table, in front of him. "It's right there in front of you. A billion dollars. Take it. You're the big hero who nailed Steve Jobs."

"There's no point in you doing this."

"*Au contraire*," I say. "There is most definitely a point. You know what the point is? To find out what you're after. And now I know. I've offered you a billion dollars to settle this, and you've said no. Obviously you're not interested in settling this. You want a big trial. You want the free publicity. You want to launch a political career, and you're drafting on my celebrity to get yourself some attention. That's what I'm comprehending. And that's what I'm going to say when the Wall Street analysts and the media start calling me and asking me what's going on. I'm going to tell them I offered to pay a fine of one billion dollars, and you refused."

"I can't believe you'd come in here making threats," Doyle says.

"Well, believe it," I say. "Because I'll roll right over you, you fuckwit."

He starts sputtering. "You of all people," he says. "Facing the kind of trouble you're facing."

"You're jealous," I say. "You're jealous of me because I'm

richer than you, and I'm smarter than you, and I'm better than you. That's what this is all about, right? You're jealous. How sad is that?"

"I don't think you appreciate who I am, and what I can do," he says.

"And I don't think you realize what will happen if I'm prevented from developing new computers. Do you want a world where everyone uses Microsoft software? Do you want that on your head? Because that's what's going to happen."

"I like Windows," he says.

"You what?"

"I think Windows is great."

I'm astounded. I could fall out of my chair. Maybe this is because I live in the Bay Area, but in all of my life I've never heard anyone actually say that they liked Windows.

"You like rebooting twenty times a day?" I say. "You like having apps interfering with each other and causing the system to hang? You like having to go look up drivers? You like spyware?"

"That doesn't happen on our machines." Poon says. "And by the way, my Zune kicks the crap out of the iPod."

"Come on. Please." But then something occurs to me. "Wait a minute. Is Microsoft putting you up to this? Is that what this is about? Are they paying you? Friggin Gates. I wouldn't put it past him. Look, whatever they're paying you, I'll pay you double that."

Doyle tells Bobby, "I'm warning you right now. You need to get control of your client."

Bobby puts his hand on my arm and says we should go. At this point I shift into my pissed-off three-year-old routine: crying, shouting, pounding my fists on the table.

"You're killing me!" I say. "You're killing me! You're trying to kill me!"

Doyle stands up. Poon does too. He's smiling so hard it looks like his face is going to crack. He's loving this.

"Thanks for your time," Doyle says. "We'll be in touch."

Outside, Bobby and I stand on the steps watching traffic go by on Golden Gate. Bobby is being all weird and quiet. He hasn't said a word since we left the conference room. It's just past noon, and the plaza is filled with frigtards having their brown bag lunches and talking about last night's *American Idol,* or whatever it is that frigtards discuss at lunch. For a moment I almost feel jealous of these morons. I wonder what it would be like to be fat and oblivious and blissful, munching away on a sandwich made of cancer-causing chemical-laden cold cuts and thinking how great life is.

"Steve," Bobby says, "I'm sorry to say this, but we're going to have to rethink our arrangement."

"What, you're raising your rates now, because I'm a difficult client?"

"Um, no. Not that. I'm resigning."

"What's that supposed to mean?"

"I'm dropping you as a client. I don't handle Kevorkian cases."

"Kevorkian cases?"

"Assisted suicide. It's not my bag, baby. You need to find a different lawyer."

"Look, Bobby. I'm sorry. Okay? I'll behave better."

"No you won't. You can't. It's not in your nature. I told Tom this from the start. There's only one kind of person that I won't represent. You know what that is? Sociopaths. You know why? Not because they're evil. Because they don't take direction. They don't listen. You know what else? Every CEO I've ever met is a sociopath."

He takes a pair of Oakley sunglasses from the breast pocket of his suit jacket and slides them onto his face. He gives me a big smile, and shakes my hand. "Good luck to you," he says, and takes off down the steps, his gelled hair glistening in the sun.

No great loss. Frankly I didn't think he was doing such a hot job anyway.

One of my great strengths—maybe my greatest strength— is that I never listen to anything that anyone else says. But somehow that comment from Bobby D. about me being a sociopath gets stuck in my head. And it's bugging me. I keep asking myself, "Am I really a sociopath?" Certainly there is evidence to support this thesis. Zack Johnson hates me. My wife almost hates me. My board hates me. My management team hates me, so much that they've leased a building for me in a different city and stuck me out there by myself. Even Ja'Red refuses to work with me. He's staying at headquarters and sends me my mail by courier.

So maybe I am a sociopath. Certainly my soul has gone down a dark path. For this I blame the corrosive, karma-destroying people with whom I now must associate. In the old days my job involved hanging out with geeks and engineers, throwing parties in the parking lot on Friday night and going out for pineapple pizza and talking about microprocessors and memory caches. I loved that life. I loved making products. I loved the moment when you put together a prototype and you flip the switch and the electrons begin coursing through the circuits and suddenly, as if by magic, your machine comes to life.

But that's not my job anymore. Now my job involves flying back and forth to Los Angeles and having meaningless meetings with shitbags from the music and movie business.

Consider that the day after Bobby tells me I'm Charles Manson Junior, I'm all by myself in the Jobs Jet, zipping down to Los Angeles, where I'll ride by myself in a limousine and stay by myself in the penthouse at the Chateau. The only interactions I'll have are with people I absolutely despise. They make my skin crawl, every single one of them.

I swear they are the darkest souls on the planet. I feel nauseated just being in a room with them, having to breathe the same air as they do. I need to wash in holy water after I spend time in their presence. These aren't engineers or inventors. They don't create anything. They don't build anything. All they do is make deals. They're criminals, basically.

Worse yet, there is no point to any of these meetings. It's all a form of Kabuki theater. All of the actual work gets done by lawyers. Nevertheless, every record label boss and movie studio chief insists on having a million meet-and-greets with El Jobso, where we both have to tell each other how important the other guy is and how much we value this relationship and how important it is to build personal connections and to have respect for one another.

Of course as soon as I turn my back they lie and cheat and go back on their word. These are people who will look you in the eye and tell you something, then turn around later and swear they never said any such thing. You can spend years negotiating a deal with these sons of whores, fighting over every sentence, every word, and finally you come to an agreement and you think, "Okay, we're done." But you're not done. Signing a piece of paper means nothing. It might as well have never happened. They just keep at you, every day, pushing, cheating, pushing some more, changing the terms, trying to raise the price of songs above ninety-nine cents or to find a way to get a bigger slice for themselves. It's like being attacked by bees. You've got this swarm of crooks feeding on you.

That's how I feel every time I'm in Los Angeles. These guys are like a cross between Tony Soprano, Bill Gates, and the monster from *Alien*. Even when you catch them cheating they don't apologize. They just move on to the next swindle. And they're really good at it, because they've been doing it for so long. They've spent decades practicing on recording artists and actors and screenwriters. But their biggest skill doesn't involve being extremely sly or clever—it's simply having the balls to be brazen and shameless and just plain awful. They're like guys who steal purses from old ladies. It's not that it's hard to do, but what kind of person does it? This is the movie business. This is the music business. They've been operating this way for so long that they don't know any other way to behave.

This trip to Los Angeles begins with a meeting at Disney. First Iger has to spend thirty minutes giving me grief about the Pixar options stuff. Then we have a meeting with Michael Jackson, who is shopping around a superhero movie called *Holy Man*. Disney has no intentions of ever making this movie, but Iger and his guys thought it would be hilarious to hear Michael make his pitch. Twenty top Disney execs are sitting around a table, and Michael's Fruit of Islam bodyguards are assembled all around the edges of the room. Then Tito comes in and does a big introduction and goes, "Ladies and gentlemen, I give you . . . Holy Man!"

In walks Michael wearing a red cape and black tights and a blue shirt with a white H on it. He explains that he will play a character called Holy Man who is born on Earth but is really a divine being from another planet, and who is called upon to save the Earth from an evil villain.

Iger, with a straight face, says, "Michael, um, since the character's name is Holy Man, how would you feel about having the costume have holes in it? Wouldn't that make sense?"

Michael gets exasperated and says, "Bob, it's not that kind of holy, okay? It's holy as in, you know, like God. Like holy."

The Disney dicks are snickering and kicking each other under the table. Michael appears not to notice. Iger goes, "I see, okay, my bad. Sorry. Continue."

Michael says this is guaranteed to be the biggest movie of all time, so he wants fifty million dollars in cash before shooting begins and twenty percent of the gross receipts.

"Look, you white devils, I grew up in this business. I know all of your dirty white devil tricks. If you won't meet my terms I'll walk across the street and get some other batch of white devils to bankroll me. You have twenty-four hours to give me an answer."

He snaps his fingers and does his little Michael Jackson sideways kick thing. His crew takes off in formation. The Disney guys burst out laughing, then wander back to their offices where they will spend the rest of the day pretending to check email or make phone calls or whatever it is that passes for work in Hollywood.

49

Worse yet is my afternoon meeting with Ivan Arsim at Massive Records. This meeting was set up months ago, for reasons neither of us can remember. There is no point to it, since we already carry their music on iTunes. But it's on our calendars, so here we are. Ivan is an enormous guy from the Bronx who started out promoting rappers. Then he launched a music label which got bought by one company which was bought by another company and now here he is, the top executive at a publicly traded company with a market value of three billion dollars, sitting in an office on the thirtieth floor of a glass tower in Los Angeles with a marble desk and big plasma screens everywhere and loads of gold records hanging on the walls.

He's six-foot-five and all muscle, with close-cropped hair and a permanent tan, a shiny black shirt and black suit, thick gold chain around his neck and another at his wrist. The first time I met him I thought he was one of the bodyguards. He looks like he should be working as a bouncer at a club. Or a repo man.

To be sure, the other top music executives aren't any better. Tommy Mottola? Every time he opens his mouth I have to fight the urge to burst out laughing. Then you've got the rap guys, who are just ridiculous. You talk business, and then if you want to buy a Glock or an eight-ball of coke on the way out they can take care of that too. Even the older guys who supposedly are more professional really aren't much different once you scratch the surface. They just speak better English and know how to hold a knife and fork.

So here's Ivan, who supposedly once beat a guy into a coma, wearing a Brioni suit and a very big shiny stupid wristwatch and crossing his legs to show off his hideously ugly custom-made Olga Berluti shoes. Yes, Ivan takes himself very seriously, so we all have to pretend to take him seriously too.

"So," he says.

We're sitting on leather couches in his office. A girl comes in with a cart bearing bottles of Bling H$_2$0 water, which costs forty dollars a bottle and was invented by a guy in Hollywood so that people like Ivan could feel important.

"You like this water, right? I remember from last time."

"Sure," I say.

"It's the best water there is," he says.

"Right."

"You want something else instead?"

"This is fine," I say. "Thanks."

He sits back, satisfied that I've been suitably impressed.

"So." He lays his big gorilla arm across the back of his couch. He drums his fingers. "How's business."

"Great," I say. "You?"

"Fantastic. Never better."

That's a lie, but I'm not going to call him on it. Fact is, the music companies are in a dying business, and they know it. Sure, they act all cool because they hang around with rock stars. But beneath all the glamour these guys are actually operating two very low-tech businesses. One is a form of banking, though it's really more like loan-sharking: They put up money to make records, and then they force recording artists to pay the money back, plus loads of interest. The other business is distribution. They've got big warehouses and they control the shipment of little plastic boxes that happen to have music in them. We've seen what the Internet has done to music retailers. Next to go are the big stupid warehouses. The label guys know it, which is why these bastards are fighting like cornered rats.

This is also why I try to be exceedingly polite and humble and respectful around music business guys and why I have to make stupid, pointless courtesy calls to cavemen like Ivan. As awful as it is to actually sit in the same room and breathe the same air as this guy, it's necessary. It's a performance. My method is simply to go all Zen and say as little as possible. If they ever try to talk business with me I say things like, "Let's let the lawyers hammer out the details." The idea is to keep them all feeling very important while we gradually redirect their industry's profit stream so it flows to us instead of to them.

"Question for you," Ivan says.

"Shoot."

"The parent company is doing a reorg, and they're gonna give me a new title. What's better, CEO or chairman? Which should I be?"

"That's easy. CEO. Definitely. The CEO is the guy who runs the company. The chairman is just a figurehead."

"But the chairman's above the CEO, right?"

"Not really."

"Well why did Sinatra call himself the chairman of the board? He wasn't the CEO, he was chairman."

"Well," I say, "you've got a point there."

"Yeah. I'm gonna be Chairman." He stands up. I guess this means our meeting is over. "Thanks for coming by, Steve. I think we've really got a really synergistic arrangement that's, uh, mutually beneficial to, uh, to both of us, right? It's a win-win for everybody."

I'm halfway out the door when he says, "Jeez, I almost forgot. There's something I was gonna tell you. I heard you're trying to get the Beatles to sign up for iTunes, only the dragon lady is giving you hassles."

"Basically."

"I've got an idea for you. You got a minute? Come back and sit down. I think you're gonna like this."

Dinner with a movie studio boss rounds out my wonderful day in Los Angeles. Jake Green is the head of Poseidon Films. They've made some of the biggest movies in Hollywood history, and we've been trying to get their archives onto iTunes for years. But all we do is meet and talk, meet and talk. We'll agree on something, and I'll fly home, and two weeks later I'll find out nothing has happened. Whoever we dealt with isn't there anymore and now we have to start over with someone else.

Jake is a small guy with gray eyes and what appears to be an expensive manicure. He speaks very, very quietly, so you have to lean in to hear him. He's very polished. Knows exactly what wine to order. But I've always heard that beneath the veneer he's a total hard case. He grew up in Detroit and came up in the music business, booking bands. Then he started distributing films, just weirdo B-movie stuff, sci-fi and horror. From there he got into bankrolling pictures himself. A couple of them hit it big, and now he's running a major. In all our meetings I've never seen the tough side of him. He's always been a complete gentleman. He even does yoga, or so he says.

After dinner we're walking to the limo, which is parked down the street, and on the way we get approached by a very aggressive homeless guy. Jake tenses up but I'm like, "Hey, let me handle this." I whip out an iPod Shuffle and give it to the guy. I do this all the time. It's part of my belief that music has the power to transform people's lives. I always carry a handful of Shuffles with me, pre-loaded with Dylan and Joan Baez, stuff like that, which I give out to homeless people. Usually these folks just fall speechless and start being all grateful.

Not this guy. He goes, "Hey man, what'm I sposeta do with this thing?" I try to explain what it is and he goes, "Fuck you, jack-off, I know what the fuck it is, and lemme axe you sumfin'. Can I smoke this thing? Will it get me high? No. It will not. Now I need some *crack*, okay? I need to smoke some goddamn crack, right now. So gimme some goddamn fucking green cash money so I can buy some goddamn crack."

We keep walking, and I tell him that we don't have any money but he should listen to the Shuffle, and if not, it's worth a lot of money, so maybe he could sell it. The guy starts working on Jake, saying, "Hey man, tell your yuppie friend not to be so cheap, man, tell your buddy give me some money."

Jake won't look at the guy or even acknowledge him, which only gets the guy more pissed off. Finally we get to the limousine and the guy starts going on about how we must be fucking millionaires and yet we won't even help him out with a few bucks.

"Don't tell me you ain't got no money, you riding in a car like this, so gimme some fucking change, man, or better yet, gimme twenny bucks so I can go buy a rock. Come on, man, gimme a twenny so I can go get me some crack."

We start to get into the car when out of nowhere, the guy produces a knife. Not a big one, but a knife nonetheless.

Jake sees this and hurries around the car, saying, "Okay, sir, look, now, wait, hold on, okay? Just hold on. We'll help you out, okay? We'll give you some money."

He reaches into his pocket as if he's going to take out some money, but instead he does this little karate-type move, whack-whack-whack. The knife falls out of the guy's hand and clatters onto the pavement. Jake grabs him by the head, spins him around and snaps his neck. Bam. He's down and he's not getting up. Because his head is now screwed on sideways, looking out over his shoulder, and his tongue is hanging out of his mouth, and his eyes are rolled up in his head.

Jake says, "Get in the car. Don't talk. Just get in the car. Let's go."

We drive off, saying nothing. After a few minutes Jake says, in this tight voice, "So that never happened, right?"

I point out to him that someone could have seen us and called the cops, or that the guy might have some friends who'll come looking for him, and for sure people are going to find the body there and they'll know there was a limo parked there. My left knee is bouncing up and down. I can't control it. I feel like I might throw up.

"We can call the cops ourselves," I say. "We'll tell them what happened. The guy came at me with a knife. It was self-defense. You saved my life. I'll back you up on that."

Jake says, "Hey. Look. Do we have a problem here? Do we? 'Cause if we do, I gotta know that right now."

He waits. I say nothing. He's glaring at me. He's got these dead black eyes. Then he goes, "I'm gonna ask you again. That never happened, right?"

I look down at my hands. "I don't even know what you're talking about," I say.

"Good. Very good. Okay. Well, that was a very nice restaurant, wasn't it? I should not have had that dessert though. I'm going to regret that tomorrow on the treadmill. Well, anyway. Thank you for an enjoyable evening. I'm really looking forward to doing business together."

When I get to the hotel I call Larry and tell him what happened. He's up at his house in Malibu, where I was supposed to stay on this trip, except at the last minute Larry called and told me I was still welcome to stay over but he was coming to Los Angeles and he was going to be having a three-way with two girls he met on Craigslist, and he knows that kind of thing makes me uncomfortable, especially since it might involve what Larry refers to as "some heavy shit." So Ja'Red called the Chateau and they moved Harvey Weinstein into the smaller penthouse, which I'll admit is kind of satisfying.

Larry insists that Jake did not really kill any homeless guy, and that the whole thing was a fake. He swears he heard a story about Jake doing the exact same thing in front of someone else.

"It's a psych-out," he says. "Makes him look like a tough guy. He's trying to intimidate you. He's fucking with your head. Plus you feel indebted to him, because he protected you. I know it's fucked up. But that's how everything is in Los Angeles. It's all an act. That homeless guy was probably some actor, working for free so he can get a part in some movie." "The guy's head was on sideways," I say.

"So maybe a stunt man. They can do stuff like that. Trust me, as soon as you drove off the guy got up and walked away. It was all staged. Come on, these are movie guys. It's what they do." He takes a deep hit off a joint and holds it. "How you doing otherwise?"

I'm not quite sure how to answer that. I just sigh and say nothing.

"What?" he says.

"I'm tired," I say. "I'm feeling old."

"You and me both, brother."

"You got the two girls there?"

"They're tied up in the dungeon room. I'm taking a break."

After we hang up I go out on the terrace and sit looking out at the lights of Los Angeles. All I have to do is be patient, and eventually all of this will be mine. The movie business, the music business. All of it.

Then I think of the meetings I have scheduled for tomorrow, and how much I dread them. I try to imagine doing this job for another ten years. Or even one year. I don't think I can do it.

In my bag I still have the card that Matt, the CIA guy, left with me. I fetch my phone to dial his number, but just as I pick up the phone it begins to buzz.

It's Mrs. Jobs. She wants to know how I'm doing. She says she's sorry for yelling at me, and if I really want to flee the country, she'll go with me. Which, oddly enough, makes me not want to flee after all.

"Let's hang in there," I say. "We'll give it a little more time."

51

"**Have you seen it?**" Ja'Red says. He's sitting behind his desk looking like a kid on Christmas morning. I'm back at headquarters for the first time since my banishment to Palo Alto. I've been told only that I should be prepared for a huge surprise. For all I know this will involve FBI agents and handcuffs. But now, seeing the smile on Ja'Red's face, I don't think so.

"It's incredible," he says. "It's like . . . it's like looking into the face of God."

I go into my office. Lars Aki is there, beaming. Beside him is Mike Dinsmore, so pale he seems to be glowing.

"It's done," Lars says.

He hands me a box—a beautiful glossy black box made of heavy cardboard and hinged on the back like a jewelry case. Inside, cushioned in black velvet, is the iPhone. They're right. It's beautiful. Silver and black, with rounded edges. It's the most beautiful object I've ever seen. I take it out of the case, and hold it in my hand. It is sleek and thin and light. But solid. Like a piece of really well-crafted jewelry. Perfect.

"Turn it on," Lars says.

"It works?"

He nods. I press the power button—which, because of the incredibly intuitive design, I am able to identify without reading a manual. The screen blinks and lights up. The phone comes to life. Icons fill the screen.

Tears begin streaming down my face. I can't help it. I turn to the window.

"All those people," I say. "Billions of them. The whole world. They have no idea what is coming. This product—this changes everything."

"Everything," Lars says, nodding.

"The world," Mike Dinsmore says, "will never be the same."

Mike looks at me. I look at him. All of the bad blood, all of the fighting, all of the heartaches and struggles are behind us now. I reach out to him. We embrace. Then Lars joins in too. For a long time the three of us just stand there, holding each other in a three-way man hug. It's one of the most powerful moments of my life.

November flies by in a blur. I'm totally back in charge again, running things at headquarters, putting in long hours in planning meetings and putting the finishing touches on our advertising and marketing campaign around the iPhone.

Up in San Francisco, Doyle has convened a grand jury, or so we've been told. The whole thing is top secret, and frankly I can't be bothered to worry about it. For now they're leaving me alone, and that's all I care about. Our sales are going crazy. Every morning I get a report that rolls up our business from the day before, breaking things down by make and model and market—iPods in India, iMacs in Brazil, whatever. Everything's booming. There's not a weak spot in the lineup.

On Thanksgiving we've got a big crowd: Larry and Mrs. Larry; Bono and The Edge; Sting and Trudie Styler; Tom Bowditch; Lars Aki and some guy named Michael that he met at a club; Al Gore, who's on the outs with Tipper because she says he's "gone Hollywood" and so he's living in California for the time being, and wearing sandals letting himself get fat again; Ja'Red and his girlfriend, the smoothie maker slash modern dancer; Sergey Brin from Google and his Uncle Fetya, who arrived in a bus with a dozen Stanford coeds.

We put out a big spread, with Tofurky and butternut squash and cranberry sauce and three kinds of brown rice, followed by organic apple pie with soy-based ice cream, then some digestion yoga in the backyard. It's a totally intense and eclectic salon-type gathering with loads of really brilliant conversation and philosophical debates over huge issues like net neutrality and the long tail theory and the patent system and digital rights management.

The highlight of the evening comes when I break out some iPhones, which everyone just raves about, except for The Edge, who has had a wee bit too much to drink and is asleep outside in a lawn chair, and Uncle Fetya, who seems to believe the iPhone is a miniature television and hands it back in disgust after Sergey, in Russian, explains that he cannot change the channel to a Russian-language station.

During the first week of December I fly into New York on a snowy day to meet with Yoko Ono at her apartment in the Dakota. This time she actually keeps the appointment, and she's as crazy as ever. We're drinking green tea on the floor of her living room and watching snow pile up on the window ledges and she's acting all Zen and telling me how she prays for my soul and how she's glad that my Apple and "the real Apple" are trying to make peace.

"I know this is what John would have wanted," she says. "He cared so much about peace. Not war, but peace. Yes. That was John's way. And so it is mine as well."

She insists, as she has before, that if we put Beatles music up on iTunes the band must be called "John Lennon and the Beatles" and that Yoko Ono must be listed as a member of the group, even on the early albums, which were recorded before John met her.

But then she tells me she's opposed to the iTunes deal altogether, because she believes the Internet is an unholy space filled with pornography and sexual deviants. She also says it would be wrong for John's music to be "smashed into these tiny bits and sprayed around on these wires."

I explain that it's just a distribution deal, just like when the Beatles put out their music on cassette tapes, and eight-track tapes, and compact discs.

"It's just a new format," I tell her.

"But it is an evil format. This Internet, I don't like it. It is not human. John was against computers. I am against them too. I do not allow them in my home. You see, they are not good things, Steven. I say this with all respect, but to me you represent everything that is evil about the modern world. Not only with music. You have cheapened movies too, by making them with computers. These are machines, Steven. These are not human. And the stories you tell in your movies, these do not uplift people. They only pander."

I tell her I'm a little bit taken aback by this criticism, considering that it's coming from a woman who once hung pictures of a giant vagina all over Liverpool.

"That was one of my favorite installations," she says. "The vagina is so beautiful, don't you think? It is where all of us enter the world. You should make a Pixar children's movie about a vagina. It would be a tribute to motherhood."

She starts going on for the millionth time about how she wants to guard John's legacy and what a precious gift to the world John was. Yoko's thing is just to repeat things over and over in a monotone voice, to wear you down. It's a Japanese business tactic; they all do it. For a while I'm just agreeing with everything she says and trying to be all Zen about it, and Yoko is giving me the Zen right back, and we're both working our Zen and trying to be more passive aggressive and monotone and repetitive than the other one.

But then I take her in a different direction—down the route that Ivan Arsim recommended. To be honest, even when I walked in the door today I wasn't sure I would do this. But here we are.

"There's something I have to tell you," I say, in my softest Zen-master voice. "I want you to hear it from me rather than from someone else. I'm buying the catalog from Sony."

She knows what I mean. I'm talking about the publishing catalog that Michael Jackson bought twenty years ago and then sold to Sony. Yoko has been trying to buy it for years, but Sony wants a billion and a half dollars and she doesn't have that kind of money.

"We're going to record the songs all over again, fresh, using all digital equipment, so it's totally high resolution. Way better than CD quality. It's so exciting. Paul's going to take the lead on the project. He's got Ringo signed up to do the drum tracks. Paul says he can play the guitar parts himself, or we can get guest stars to do some tracks. Eric Clapton wants to get involved. George Martin says he'll produce."

She smiles. "This is a wonderful fantasy," she says, "but I'm afraid it is quite impossible."

She's trying to look all Zen and detached and bemused, as if I'm some lunatic proposing that we should all go live on the moon. But I can see in her eyes that she's freaked out.

"Actually," I say, "Paul says it's very doable."

In fact that's only half true. Paul did look into it, but there are some questions about legal issues. At the very least Yoko could turn herself into a very huge pain in the ass, which as we all know is something she very much likes to do. So we're bluffing. Nevertheless Paul says he'll back me up on this and that we should push Yoko as hard as we have to. He's dying to sell the songs on iTunes. And he hates Yoko even more than I do.

"Paul is a fool," she says. "He has no talent. He never had any talent. John always said that. John was the soul of the Beatles. Without John there is no Beatles. And you won't have John."

"Well, see, that's the beauty of it. Paul and George Martin have got all these old master tapes, and we can take John's voice off those tapes. Granted, he'll sound like shit compared to the other voices, because his recordings will be grainy and low quality. But we can alter his voice with digital tools."

"No," she says. "No digital tools. John was opposed to digital."

"John died before digital recording was invented."

"But he saw it coming. He told me he would never do this."

"Well, the fall-back is that Paul says he can just sing John's parts."

That does it. Now she's left her Zen behind and she's just plain furious.

"Paul is a criminal. Paul stole John's work and presented it as his own. Now he's going to do this? I hate Paul. I always did. This is a ridiculous project. What's the point? It would take years record all these songs all over again."

"Five years," I say. "We've worked out the schedule. We'll have different teams working all around the world and sharing files over the Internet. Paul will be the artistic director overseeing the project. And yes, it's daunting, but think about how much money we'll make. Do you have any idea how popular these albums will be?"

"I'm sure that appeals to Paul. He loves money. More than anything else he loves money."

"But the beauty is that there's also such great artistic merit to the project. It's way better than just re-releasing the old songs for downloads. You've said it yourself, people already own these songs. Why buy them again? But this? This would be all new material. This would be the songs recorded the way they were meant to be recorded. This will become the new definitive Beatles catalog. It's not just about the money. Paul says that with a lot of John's songs he always hated the way John mixed them, and he's been dying to take another crack at them."

"That's outrageous. That's a sacrilege. I will not allow this. Absolutely not."

"I'm afraid there's not much you can do."

"You cannot record John Lennon's songs without John Lennon."

"Well, see, you can, actually. That's why I'm buying the catalog. I'll own the rights, so then I can license the rights to Paul. And to myself, actually, because I'm going to get involved as a co-producer."

"You really would do this?"

"I intend to do it."

"You said you loved John."

"I do love him. More than anyone in all of history."

This is true, sort of. Sometimes it's John Lennon, though more often it's Dylan. I go back and forth. But there's no sense splitting hairs at a moment like this.

"You even wear glasses like his."

"Yes," I say. "As a tribute to him."

"Yet you would do this to him? To his memory? You would spend a billion and a half dollars to buy the catalog, and then spend years in a studio, and you would erase John Lennon from the Beatles, just to spite me?"

"It's not about spite. It's about the money. The stuff we're talking about goes way beyond this project with Paul. There's huge interest in the catalog from other artists. The whole asset has just been terribly underutilized at Sony. You can't believe the offers they've had, and they've always turned them down because they don't think they're classy enough. Britney Spears wants to do an album of all-girl Beatles duets with guest stars like Madonna and Christina Aguilera. Garth Brooks wants to do country-western Beatles. Snoop Dogg and P. Diddy want to do a Beatles hip-hop album. Then there are the advertising deals. The Stones have been all over that market. But the Beatles? Nowhere to be seen. On commercials alone I'll earn back my investment in two years. You know the company that makes Depends? Those adult diapers? They want to use "When I'm Sixty-Four" as an ad jingle. So do Viagra and Cialis and Levitra. They're all bidding against each other. There's just huge interest, and it's never been exploited."

I let that last word hang in the air. I chose it on purpose. We sit there in silence. She's beaten, and she knows it.

Finally she says, in a soft voice, "Let me understand you. If I permit you to have the digital rights, you will drop this threat of desecrating John's memory? You will not re-record the songs?"

"There wouldn't be much point in distributing two versions," I say.

"I see. Well." She toys with her cup of tea. Her bottom lip begins to quiver. "It appears I am in an impossible position. I am placed between two bad choices."

She sighs, and puts her hands to her face, and starts to sob. I start thinking about all the shit this poor woman has been put through in her life. No wonder she's so friggin nuts. I suppose she's thinking that too. Or maybe she's thinking about John. She starts to shiver, and shake. Her shoulders are heaving. When she looks up at me her mascara is running and her face is streaked with black tears. For a tiny moment I feel a flicker of guilt about doing this to the widow of the person I sometimes admire more than anyone else in the world. But this is my job. This is my fate. Because of who I am, because of what I do, this nasty piece of work has fallen to me.

"I was right about you," she says. "You are an evil man."

"I suppose I am."

"Please go," she says.

The lifts in the Dakota are the old-fashioned kind, rickety and slow-moving, with glass-paned wooden doors and an operator who drives the car with a brass shift lever. The operator is a squat, ugly old man dressed in a bellman's uniform and cap. He smells of liquor. He eyes me but says nothing. The old lift grumbles and groans its way down through the floors. The wooden floor creaks. The light flickers. I close my eyes and feel myself descending. I think about Yoko, sprawled out on the floor, crying. For a moment I have the sense that this monkey-faced bellman is taking me not to the lobby, but farther still, down through the basement, down through the sewers, all the way down into hell. And you know what? I wouldn't blame him. It's what I deserve.

53

Outside, night is falling. Big snowflakes, as fat as goose down, swirl around the streetlamps. Yellow cabs race down the street, tires whooshing in the slush. Across the street, in Central Park, kids are firing snowballs at each other. I'm flashing back to the years when I had an apartment in the San Remo, two blocks from here. I'm remembering being twenty-eight years old, newly wealthy, and going outside in a snowstorm like this with Sabrina Gould, the actress, on a night when the whole city seemed to have slowed to a halt. We walked along Central Park West, right where I am now. It was midnight and there was no sound at all, just the crunch of our boots in the snow.

"Gosh, I remember that too," Sabrina says a few minutes later when I arrive at her apartment. She's still living in the city, tucked away like a piece of jewelry in a posh building on Fifth Avenue, a few blocks up from our retail store. In the ten years since I saw her last she has gone through two husbands, both of them super-rich Wall Street douchebags, both of them at least twenty years her senior. Big settlements have allowed her to disappear from the world and to live like a tsarina. Her apartment takes up the top two floors of the building and is wrapped by a balcony that is itself bigger than most apartments. From where we're sitting, in her living room, we have a view out over the East River and all the way down to the bottom of Manhattan.

"I've married well," Sabrina says, "and divorced better."

She's never in the tabloids, never on the news. She travels wherever she wants and does whatever she pleases and is left alone by the media. She hasn't made a movie in fifteen years and swears she has no interest in ever making one again.

"Do you have any idea what I'd have to do if I wanted to make a movie now?" she says in her Southern drawl, which sounds like honey and bourbon mixed in a glass. "The dieting, the plastic surgery. Just so I can play Batman's girlfriend in some teenage jerkoff comic book fantasy? No thanks. Honestly I think the best thing that has ever come along in the movie business is this computer generated imagery stuff. Pretty soon y'all will just create characters with your computers and leave us poor human beings alone."

"No computer," I say, "will ever create a woman who looks like you."

"True. But you know what I mean." The great thing about Sabrina is that she knows she's gorgeous, and she just accepts it. It's simply a fact, like the fact that she's tall, and that she's half Irish, and that she grew up in Tennessee. She's got this gorgeous curly black hair, green eyes, a little spray of freckles across the bridge of her nose. Age hasn't diminished her looks; if anything she's more beautiful than when I was dating her.

"Here's the thing," she says. "I'm fifty-two years old, I've had no work done, I'm ten pounds overweight, and I'm happy. I see my old friends who are still in the business and my heart breaks for them. They're out there in Los Angeles starving themselves for years at a time, mutilating themselves with plastic surgery. They look like monsters. Do you know why so many of them end up as activists for animal rights? It's because they identify with the poor little minks and veal calves. They're *projecting*, you see? They don't dare to speak up about how the movie business treats actresses. So they join PETA and crusade for the poor little bunny rabbits in their cages. Because that's who they are, Steve. Poor little bunnies, penned up in their mansions in the Hollywood hills, not allowed to eat. God, it's awful."

I tell her about my meetings in Los Angeles, about Jake Green from Poseidon murdering the homeless guy.

"That's why I got out of the business," she says. "I hated the people. Even more than that, I hated the person that I was becoming. I was becoming one of them."

I tell her about my meeting with Yoko Ono, and how I just strong-armed her into letting me sell Beatles songs on iTunes. "I feel like shit," I say.

"You should feel like shit," she says. "That's terrible."

"It was awful. The look on her face. I couldn't believe I was doing it to her. I felt like the devil."

"Yeah." She looks down at the glass in her hands. She rolls the ice around in it. "Honey," she says, "you need to do some thinking." Then she looks up and gives me this bright smile and says, "Hey, you know what? Let's go out. There's a place I want to take you. Are you hungry?"

It's a hole in the wall, uptown in Spanish Harlem, where the specialty is roasted chicken and you order either half a chicken or a whole chicken and they serve it with rice and beans, a basket of tortillas, and wedges of lime. Sabrina orders a half chicken and eats all of it along with a Mexican beer. I get a plate of rice and beans, yucca and plantains. The place is crowded, noisy, lots of Spanish being spoken, Mexican music on the stereo, Frida Kahlo and Diego Rivera prints on the wall.

"So have you noticed?" Sabrina says, when we're finishing our flan and coffee. I shrug. The only thing I've noticed is that there's a cockroach sitting up on the counter next to the cash register, perched there like a pet. The hostess is ringing up customers and making no effort at all to chase it away.

"Nobody knows who we are," she says. "None of the waiters, none of the customers. They've never heard of you. They've never seen my movies, or if they have, they don't recognize me.

It's like we're invisible. Do you realize we're going to have to pay for this meal? How cool is that?"

"It's not like the old days." Back when we were dating we would arrive at a club, or a restaurant, and they'd clear a path for us and give us some special table and we'd never get billed for anything. It was all part of Sabrina's job—half of these places had made deals with her movie studio, or paid off her manager, so that she'd show up and stay for an hour or two and let herself be photographed going in and out.

"Do you remember when we had to have my publicist put out a statement denying that we were dating, even though we were? Because I was supposed to be dating—who was it? Someone gay. I can't remember."

"Jimmy Nelson," I say. "You were in a movie with him."

"Poor Jimmy. He's dead. Did you know that? Killed himself."

"I remember seeing something in the papers."

"His agent dropped him. He couldn't get work. Poor guy. He didn't want to be a has-been."

"Who does?"

"You know what? It's great being a has-been. The whole thing about being famous, whatever that means, well, the price you pay for that, the chunks it takes out of you, it's just not worth it. People don't appreciate anonymity. It's great, honestly. You should consider it."

"As a matter of fact," I say, "I am."

I explain my situation with the feds. She claims she hasn't heard anything about it. I find that hard to believe. She says she never reads the newspaper. Maybe she's just being polite. I tell her about Francis X. Doyle, and about Tom Bowditch and his crazy plan to zip me out of the country and off to someplace in the South Pacific.

"That sounds marvelous," she says.

"You think? I'm afraid I'll go nuts if I stop working."

"Life is short. You've done plenty."

Outside, my car is waiting. We ride downtown in silence. At her building she asks if I want to come inside. I know what this offer means. And I'll admit, I think about it. I really do. But in the end I tell her I'd better not. Truth is, I've never been a big lady killer type. Even when I was single, I wasn't all that interested in getting laid. Larry used to call me "Gandhi" because I wouldn't go out and chase pussy with him. Now he's on his fourth marriage and he's still the biggest gash hound I've ever known. It's like a disease. In my case it's not that I'm some nice guy. It's just that I never found other people all that interesting. At least not enough to be worth putting that much effort into. I've had feelings for people, sure. But not love, really. The only person I've ever felt that for was myself.

"You're a sweetie," she says, and kisses me on the cheek. I wait at the curb and watch her go into the building. At the glass doors she stops and turns and waves to me. It occurs to me that given our ages and the infrequency of our get-togethers, it's almost certain that we will never see each other again in this lifetime. A chill runs through me. I imagine myself as Sabrina must see me—an old man, small and gray-haired, weary, bespectacled, bundled in a heavy black coat in the back of a big black car, obscured by foggy glass and falling snow, a small face growing smaller as the car surges into the street and disappears into the traffic.

Back in the Valley, things are rocking. Every day we're blowing through our sales projections. Our biggest challenge is finding extra capacity at our manufacturing plants in China so we can keep up with demand—and all I can think about is those poor kids who now are going to have to work even longer hours. On the bright side, our stock price keeps ticking up, and even as it does the Wall Street analysts keep recommending it more. One of these guys is quoted in the *Wall Street Journal* calling us "the Sony of the twenty-first century" and saying we're "the one stock that everyone should own and hold and keep in a box. It'll put your kids through college." I don't celebrate Christmas, because I don't believe in Christianity, but if I did this would be the best present I could ever hope to get.

Naturally this run of good luck is all too good to be true. On Christmas Day, while the Jobs clan is sitting around the house non-celebrating, I get a call from Tom Bowditch informing me that good old Charlie Sampson has found even more bad news—it's like Chinese water torture, I swear—and the board will be meeting the next day to get a full report.

When I arrive, a half hour late, Sampson is already sitting in my spot at the head of the conference table.

"I thought you were done," I say.

"Funny," he says, "I was just about to say the same to you."

Nobody laughs. Sampson points to an empty chair down at the far end of the table. Whatever. He's trying to annoy me. I won't give him the satisfaction. The whole management team is here, as well as the whole board of directors, including Al Gore, who has actually made an appearance in person. Everyone looks super pissed because they're all supposed to be hanging out with their families at Vail or Aspen or Hawaii or whatever, and I'm like, "Hey, don't be mad at me, I'm not the one who called a meeting during the holidays."

Sampson launches into his presentation. His team has put together a report to send to the SEC. They've found all sorts of misdeeds and shenanigans, the worst of which is that a few years ago Sonya and some other lawyers on her team signed some documents saying that the board had held a meeting to vote on some backdated shares when in fact no such meeting occurred. This last bit has been leaked to some obscure legal magazine, which is threatening to run a story saying we engaged in forgery.

"Forgery?" I say. "I mean, isn't that just a wee bit overdramatic? I mean, just because someone signs someone else's name to a document, I don't think that's forgery."

"Actually," Sampson says, "that's pretty much the definition of forgery."

"So if I give my wife my credit card in a restaurant and she signs my name, that's a crime?"

"It's a crime," he says, "if there is an intent to deceive. You created the impression that a board meeting had occurred and that a vote had taken place, when in fact this didn't happen. That misled shareholders."

"They were going to vote for it anyway. Why drag everyone out here and make them waste an entire day just so they can raise their hands and say yes?" I turn to Al Gore. "It would be a waste of fuel, right? Isn't that what we say here, that we were trying to save the planet from global warming, and we're cutting back on travel and doing some of our meetings in virtual space? We can give it a name, like GreenMeet. Or iGreen. The iGreen Initiative."

"You lied to shareholders," Sampson says. "That's against the law."

"The laws suck. The laws need to be rewritten."

"Enough," Tom says. "Right now we've got to think about the story that's going to hit. Ross?"

Ross Ziehm says his guys have managed to stall the reporter by swearing to him that he's got it wrong and he's going to look like an idiot if he publishes this, which of course is every egomaniac reporter's worst nightmare. But Ross is not sure how long they can hold the guy off.

"We also can't figure out who's leaking," Ross says. "There's no way this stuff should be getting out."

"Get Moshe to put a team on it," Tom says. "We're not going to tolerate leaks. Whoever's leaking, I want the guy's balls on a plate."

Paul glances at me, and raises an eyebrow. I shake him off.

"Meanwhile," Tom says, "we're going to get ahead of everything by putting out our own report. We put our own spin on it. Ross?"

"Right," Ross says. "We're releasing the news this Friday, same day as we file it with the SEC. We'll put out a release at the end of the day West Coast time, after everyone back East has left for the New Year's weekend. Basically our premise is this: Did illegal activities occur? Yes. Was Steve in charge at the time? Yes. Did Steve authorize the illegal activities? Yes. Did Steve benefit from them? Yes. Therefore Steve is not responsible. Now if you don't mind, we'd like to consider this matter closed, and we ask that you leave us alone so we can go back to making the beautiful objects that restore a sense of childlike wonder to your lives."

The management team are all nodding their heads—they all get it, instinctively—but the board members look skeptical and sick to their stomachs. The old guy from the clothing store chain says, "You think that makes sense?

"Absolutely," Ross says.

"Come on. You think people are going to buy that?"

"It's all in the way you say it," Ross says. "You've just got to really *sell* it."

One thing I really admire about Ross is how smooth and patient he can be even when he's dealing with the stupidest frigtards. Me personally, I'd just tell the guy to shut up. It always cracks me up how clueless these guys on the board can be. They just don't get how things work out here in the Valley. Out here, we're the good guys. We're the guys who are making the world a better place.

"One more thing," Ross says. "If anyone gets calls from the press, you say nothing. I would expect everyone is going to get called. Just say something bland like you endorse the findings of the independent investigators, and then bounce the assholes to me. Okay? Nobody goes solo here. Nobody goes off the reservation. I want this buttoned up tighter than a nun's bunghole. And that's watertight."

Afterward, I'm in my office checking email when Tom Bowditch walks in without knocking. He comes around my desk and presses his face close to mine. He's about an inch away. His dog breath is overpowering.

"Is that still you?" he says. He's peering into my eyes.

"What are you talking about?"

He leans to the left, then to the right.

"The eyes are always the give-away," he says. "It's the one thing they never get right. Are those colored contacts? I can't see the edge of the lens."

"Have you lost your mind?"

"Just tell me," he says. "Have you gone to Scottsdale? No, wait. You're right. Don't tell me. Okay, do tell me. No. Okay. Tell me this. What's the name of the dog you had as a kid?"

"I'm allergic to dogs."

"Jesus Christ, it really *is* you. Kid, do you have rocks for brains? Why aren't you in Scottsdale?"

"I'm not going to fly off to some clinic and have some Mafia surgeon turn me into someone else," I say. "I'm not going to stage my own death and flee the country. As much as I'm sure you and your friends would like that."

He lets that slide, which means I've hit a nerve. He goes to the window and stands there, looking out.

"You know what I'm talking about," I say. "Don't you."

"Kid, you're getting boring. Look. Whatever you think you know, let me tell you what you don't know. Doyle is going to indict you. I've got someone on the inside at Doyle's office. Right after New Year's they're going to indict."

"I don't believe you."

"Fine. Don't."

"You know what I think? I think you've been trying to torpedo the stock. I think you'd like it if I stepped aside, or got killed. I think you want me to stage my own death."

He looks at me, but says nothing.

"I know about your company in the Caymans," I say.

I don't know anything, not really. It's just a guess. But, there's something about the way Tom looks today, something about his eyes. I just have this feeling, this sense of intuition.

I honestly did not believe Paul Doezen's big conspiracy theory. But I believe it now. I believe it because of the look on Tom's face. It's a dead look, a look that says he can't be bothered to keep up the ruse about us being friends. He can't even be bothered to ask me what I'm talking about, or deny what I'm accusing him of, because we both know the truth, and we're just wasting our breath talking about it.

"All right," he says, heading for the door. "I'll see you in the funny papers."

Before he can leave I say, "I can't believe it, Tom. Honestly. I thought you and I were—well, I thought the two of us were on the same side."

He stops. He stands with his back to me. He's drumming his fingers on the doorknob. For a moment it seems as if he's going to turn around and give me some big lecture about capitalism, and tell me how all my ideas, all my struggles, all my fights and failures and late nights meditating on products are nothing more than a way for people like him to make money.

But he doesn't do that. He just opens the door and walks out.

How intense is ayahuasca? Put it this way: If at some point during the trip you don't feel certain that you are dying, then you've underdosed and will need to try again some other time. But if you get it right, which we have, it's really something. The trip lasts ten to twelve hours, with side effects that include vomiting and diarrhea, so you have to wear Depends and keep a bucket beside your mat. Luckily we've got a great spirit guide, Diego, who plays a flute and keeps us centered and tells us really wild stories about how the world is going to end in the year 2012 when the Mayan calendar runs out of days.

It's New Year's Eve and we're all hanging out at Larry's Zen palace, which is a fantastic place for using psychedelics. Larry arranged the compound so that its center, a courtyard, is located directly over an energy vortex which has been compared in strength to the vortexes outside Sedona. As a result the entire courtyard possesses a really exceptional sacred energy. Diego says he's never felt anything like it, and he's from the Amazon rainforest in Peru, which is ground zero for ayahuasca ceremonies. Sting and I tripped with him down there last summer and arranged to fly him up here for the holiday. We sent the Jobs Jet to Lima to get him.

At midnight, six hours into the trip, when we're really peaking and lit up, and the vomiting and diarrhea have subsided, Diego gathers us all into a circle on the floor and starts talking about how every human being is a small power plant, a little generator, and how we all have a finite amount of energy to expend in our lifetimes, and how our lives are, unfortunately, all too brief when you consider any single individual in the context of all of space and time. He urges us to take turns talking about how we might use our energy in the year ahead. Bono talks about poverty in Africa. Sting talks about Amnesty International and ending torture. Ja'Red, who's here as my guest, talks about global warming, which is kind of lame and predictable, but he's still doing better than Larry and his Oracle guys, whose goals involve beating their sales numbers and killing companies that compete with them.

Then it's my turn, but when I begin to speak the words get choked in my throat and I feel tears welling up in my eyes. The next thing I know I've fallen off my pillow and I'm curled up into a fetal position, sobbing. It's as if all the hatred and betrayal and negative energy that I've been battling for the past six months has roared up and overwhelmed me. All the bad karma—exploiting those kids in China, throwing Zack to the wolves, dealing with all those damaged souls in Los Angeles, blackmailing Yoko Ono—it all just rolls up on me like a huge wave, crushing me.

Sting leaps in and curls up around me and spoons with me while I sob, just like I did for him last summer in the rainforest when he started thinking about global warming while he was peaking and it freaked him out.

"You've seen what they're doing to me," I say. "These bastards. These prosecutors. The press. They're having a field day."

The papers and TV shows have been filled with news about Apple all weekend, ever since we put out the press release on Friday evening. The legal journal has printed its story about the forgery, which has ignited a whole new round of outrage. Again there's the same speculation about whether I'll be forced to leave, and whether I'll face criminal charges, and whether Apple can carry on without me. Most notably, Doyle himself has been quoted hinting about the indictment that could be coming next week.

"I try to be brave," I say. "I try to pretend it doesn't bother me, that it doesn't get to me. People think that, well, you're rich, and you're a genius, so whatever, you can take it. They're so gleeful! It's like they're enjoying it! It's like they don't realize there's a human being on the other side of their abuse. Sure, a very wealthy, brilliant human being, a human being who has changed the course of history and who lives a life that these asshats could not even begin to imagine. But a human being nonetheless. With real human being feelings. And you know what? This stuff hurts. It *hurts!* I want to just go on TV and shout at these people, Look, I'm *hurting*, okay? I'm suffering! Is this enough for you? Is it? Do you want to see me bleed?"

"Easy, amigo," Sting whispers in my ear. "You're right. They're evil. We've all been through it. It's the price you pay for being an artist. You should see what they said about my last album. The madrigal songs. Terrible. Hush now, Steve. Go easy. Breathe. That's it. It's okay, Steve."

Finally I manage to gather myself and sit up. "I'm sorry," I say to the group. "I don't want to ruin the energy in the room. I'm sorry. I'm okay now."

Bono and Sting pick up guitars and start playing, softly, just finger-picking. Thing is, Bono doesn't actually play guitar all that well, and I can tell Sting is kind of pissed off, trying to show him some chords, and then they stop because one of them is out of tune, and they start doing that thing where they're tuning up, tuning down, tuning up, tuning down—yeah. Painful. The Oracle guys wander out to the kitchen for beer.

I get up and head outside to the courtyard. I need to breathe fresh air. Ja'Red comes with me. We end up sitting by the fire pit for a few hours talking about products we'd like to invent and all the cool software we'd like to write, if either of us actually knew how to write software, which we don't.

Ja'Red's eyes are blazing. I can remember being just like him, twenty-five years old and full of cool ideas and you think you're going to conquer the world. That seems like a long time ago now. For a long time we sit looking up at the stars and trying to figure out which constellation is which, and I really wish I'd learned that stuff at some point in my life, but now it's just another item to add to my list of all the things I should have done but didn't have time for because I was too busy making stupid computers.

Up above us on the hillside Larry has some super-powered telescope that supposedly cost more than the one in the Stanford observatory. Ja'Red wants to go up and look through it.

"What's the point?" I say. "You're just looking at lights. You don't know what any of it is."

"Larry said he'd take us up there. Apparently you can see Mars or something."

"Larry doesn't know what he's talking about. He's just a rich guy with a telescope, that's all."

Well, they all go hiking up the hillside anyway. They spend an hour or so up there marveling at little twinkling lights. By the time they come back it's nearly dawn, and the sky is growing pale. Ja'Red brings me a cup of herbal tea and says I really ought to cheer up, that my life isn't so bad, blah blah, mwah mwah, all the usual stuff. He says that even if they put me in jail, I'll still bounce back and be bigger than ever. "Look at Nelson Mandela," he says.

"It's not that," I say. "It's everything. The hassles. The bull-shit. The meetings. All the fighting you have to do, when all you really want to do is to make something beautiful. It should be easy, right? But it's not. It destroys your soul. That's what it comes down to, in the end. You can do this job, but you lose your soul. Not all at once, but in bits and pieces. The people you need to deal with, the things you need to do to other people—it's not healthy."

"You're tired," he says.

"I'm old," I say. "There's a difference. You'll see. Give your-self twenty-five more years."

I sip my tea. It's perfect. Delicious. I tell myself to just focus on this one perfect thing in front of me and push everything else away. But I can't.

"You know what I keep thinking about? I keep thinking about those kids in China. About what I'm doing to them."

"You're not doing anything to them," Ja'Red says.

"Yes I am. We are."

"Who? You and me?"

"You and me. All of us. All of us here. Our whole culture. You hold a music player in your hand. You have no idea that there's some kid who built it, do you? But once you do know that, once you've seen that kid, how can you keep using it? How can you do that? That's what I realized just now, when you guys were up at the telescope. I realized who it ends up hurting the most. Not them. It hurts *us*. We're the ones who suffer. We're the ones whose karma gets chewed up. We're the ones who get hurt. We're like a big organism that's really sick. We've brought it on ourselves. But we need to get well. I do. I need to get well. I'm sick. Not in my body. But in my soul."

"Dude," he says, "I agree it's not easy to be you. But you know what? You ought to stop feeling sorry for yourself. Because despite all your problems, what you don't realize is pretty much anyone in the world would *kill* to have your life. Hell, I know *I* would."

"Huh." We sit there. I sip my tea. Then it occurs to me. My solution is sitting right here, right beside me. Over the course of my life some of my greatest ideas have come to me while I was using psychedelic drugs, and this is one of the greatest ever. There's no time to waste.

"Kid," I say, "how'd you like to go for a ride in the jet?"

By the time we touch down in Scottsdale the details have been worked out. Ja'Red will get a billion dollars, plus the Jobs Jet and the Jobs Domicile, and of course the Jobs jobs, at Apple and Disney. There's no paperwork, just a verbal agreement. If there's prison time to be done after the feds are through, he does it and keeps quiet.

Five days later, when we're moved from the clinic to the safe house, Matt the male model spy is there waiting for us. He's handled the paperwork. He's lined up a private compound on an island with round-the-clock security, plus a new jet, untraceable, and a list of airports around the world where I'll have landing privileges. I'll have two billion dollars, spread out in bank accounts in different countries. The whole family will take on new names.

As for Ja'Red, there's no guarantee that he will keep his mouth shut, except that he knows that if he ever spills the beans he'll have about twelve hours to live before Matt and his friends track him down, which is a pretty good incentive. He swears he won't get cold feet, and I believe him. Why would he? The kid gets to run Apple. It's the best job in the world. Better yet, he gets to be me. He gets to stand on stage at Macworld and be worshipped like a god by people who have camped out overnight in the rain just so they can get in first and sit down front and maybe touch the hem of his robes.

That, I have to admit, is one thing I'm really going to miss.

epilogue

Yes, I was there at the Macworld conference in January. I was in the auditorium, sporting an usher's uniform and my new look. It's kind of hard to describe. Imagine Alan Arkin with a big beard and slightly Asian eyes, you'll have an idea. All morning I showed people to their seats and roamed around the hallways at the Moscone Center, even walked right up to people I knew and spoke to them—and nothing. Nobody had a clue. It's amazing what these surgeons can do.

Ja'Red, meanwhile, looked so much like me it was scary. It was like watching myself up there. The docs have aged him a bit, but he still looks great.

And he did an amazing job. He showed off the new iPhone and the Apple TV product, ran through the demos without a hitch, used his clicker, hit all of his cues.

Next day the papers and bloggers were ecstatic, saying the old Steve was back, looking tanned and rested and ready, with new energy and passion and enthusiasm. By the time those stories arrived I was already *desaparecido*, zooming off to parts unknown, where I remain today, stretched out on a lounge chair with a seventeen-inch MacBook Pro on my lap, finishing this manuscript and watching the reports about the madness surrounding the iPhone, which is going on sale today in the United States.

We call our place Casa del Fin del Mundo. Spanish is not the local language here, but Mrs. Jobs thinks it sounds cool, and I agree. We've got the offspring set up in a private school. Nobody here has any idea who we are. Even if you met me, which you might do one day, you wouldn't recognize me. You'd never even know we'd crossed paths.

I don't keep up with day-to-day stuff at Apple, though I still touch base with Ja'Red occasionally, using our amazing iChat AV videoconferencing software. Sometimes he asks for advice, though to be honest he's mostly just being nice. He doesn't need any help from me. Our December quarter was another blowout—record sales, record profits. The stock is soaring. It's up fifty percent from the start of the year, hitting new highs every week.

Of course this is great news for Ja'Red. Better yet, it has been very bad news for that traitorous butt plug Tom Bowditch. According to Ja'Red, Tom freaked out when I didn't stage a fake death. He was sitting on a huge short position, and expecting that the Death of Steve would destroy the stock price and enable him to make a killing. He hadn't anticipated the doppelganger maneuver. When the stock started going up, Tom got squeezed and was forced to cover his position. As he covered, however, he drove up the stock. So he kept having to buy at higher and higher prices. By the time the fiasco was over he'd lost a hundred million dollars. Buddha be praised.

The big indictment that was supposed to come down in January never materialized. Right now, in fact, it's looking like this backdating scandal is going to blow over, as the case against El Jobso has been falling apart. For one thing, during the past week, iPhone mania has swept the nation, and thousands of Apple faithful have taken to the streets, camping out for days so they could be the first to buy iPhones. A few days ago U.S. Attorney Francis X. Doyle had the bad luck to be walking past the Apple store in San Francisco when this madness was taking place, and I'm sorry to report that the mob recognized him, thanks in part to some flyers that Moshe Hishkill and his intelligence team may or may not have left in the area. Some say Doyle slipped while fleeing the mob and fell under a bus; others say he was pushed. Who can say? Anyway, within hours Zack Johnson and Sonya Bourne both suffered aphasic memory loss regarding their time at Apple, leaving no one to testify against me. William Poon, the Zune-using prosecutor, is long gone too; earlier this year he quit the U.S. Attorney's office and joined a law firm, to specialize in . . . wait for it . . . defending executives who've been caught up in backdating scandals.

If the charges do blow over, I'd love it if someone would find a way to hold the SEC and the U.S. Attorney accountable for their actions, for their threats and accusations and smear jobs in the press, for tarnishing my name and driving me into self-imposed exile. But I doubt this will happen. I won't hold my breath waiting for the feds to offer an apology for what they've put me through.

The truth is, I'm enjoying my time off. I've had a chance to focus on me for a change. It's been really healing for my soul. We have a full-time guru with us, Baba SunMoonStar, and every day we pray and meditate. I also spend time surfing, and doing yoga, and making lists of foods I won't eat. And I've been tackling all those heavy-duty intellectual projects that I've been putting off for so many years, like learning Japanese and reading Dante's *Inferno*.

During our last iChat Ja'Red asked me, "Dude, like, if this backdating scandal goes away or whatever, like, what are you going to do?"

I understood that what he really wanted to know was whether I planned to return. The answer is, I probably will come back—not for my sake, but for the sake of the world. Sure, maybe I'm a sociopath, as Bobby DiMarco said. I've been meditating and non-thinking about that accusation quite a bit out here, and something important has occurred to me: The world needs sociopaths. Who else ever gets anything done? Sociopaths are the ones who create, who lead, who inspire, who motivate. Was Buddha a sociopath? No doubt. Gandhi? Crazy as a loon. Same for Picasso, and Hemingway, and John Lennon. Geniuses like us may not be entirely pleasant, but let's face it, we're necessary.

So I'll probably go back, but not to Apple. For one thing, Ja'Red has turned into a really first-rate CEO. For another, I don't like what the job of running Apple has become. It's no fun anymore. I don't want to spend my time haggling with music and movie industry scumbags. I'd rather start a new company. I'll go back to my roots and do what I love most and what I do best— I'll put together a team of engineers and create the next great machine.

I'm already working on an idea that I dreamed up one day while I was sitting on the beach. I've started putting together some sketches. It's this computer built entirely out of a single sheet of touch-screen plastic that you can roll up and carry with you in a tube. All of the parts—the keyboard, the screen, the battery, the speakers—can be contained in a sheet that's only one-sixteenth of an inch thick. Some labs in Japan have been making prototypes. So far they don't really work too well, and they're prohibitively expensive. But the technology keeps getting better, and component prices are coming down. The guys in Japan say that by 2012 they'll be able to manufacture these things in large volumes for less than two thousand dollars apiece. I'm pushing them to get there by 2010.

Casa del Fin del Mundo
29 June 2007